The Big Story

The Bible as a Connected Story
for
Lent and Holy Week

by
Fay Rowland

Typeset in Century Gothic 10pt.

ISBN: 9798610630687

Acknowledgements

Thanks, as ever, go to my children for putting up with a mum who goes tappity-tappity-tap at all hours of the day and night. Mind you, as they're all teenagers now, I don't suppose they'd notice if I spent all day wrestling rhinos, as long as I served up pizza at regular intervals.

Thanks, too, to Steve, my long-suffering editor and proof-reader, who also chides me for going tappity-tappity-tap too much and tells me to get outside into God's creation for a while.

Sound advice.

Also thanks to my pet dragon, Dwagony. Not because she's been any help, but it's cool to be able to mention a dragon.

Contents

Bible Versions Used

ERV   = Easy-to-Read Version

GW   = God's Word Translation

MSG   = The Message

NCV   = New Century Version

NIV   = New International Version

NRSV   = New Revised Standard Version

WEB   = World English Bible

How to Use This Book

The Bible is one Big Story of God and God's people. This book follows the story from the very beginning up to the wonder of Easter morning.

You can follow The Big Story by yourself, with your family, in church, or in a group. The short summaries are useful for gaining an overview of the whole story of the Bible, and for showing how some familiar (and some less-familiar) parts of the Bible fit together.

You can use this book daily, weekly, or a combination of both. Each week covers a section of the Bible and finishes with the story seemingly crashing to an end, but by God's grace, it continues.

The weeks run from Mondays to Sundays, so that churches can summarise the story that week as a sermon series during Lent and Holy Week, with congregations having studied it during the previous week.

Daily

Every day includes a section of The Big Story, a space for you to respond with a question to prompt your thoughts, some Bible readings, a reflection and a short prayer. Use as many or as few of these as you prefer.

Weekly

You might like to do daily readings yourself, then meet with others during the week to discuss what you have discovered. Alternatively, you can combine all the readings for a week into one session for a weekly Bible study group or church service.

Icons

These symbols can help you to navigate to your favourite parts.

The Big Story

Today's part of the story of God and God's people. If you are in a hurry, you can simply read this and carry it with you during the day. But if you want to take things further …

Responding

Use the blank space to think about what's going on. You can jot notes, answer the question prompt, draw a picture or leave it blank – whatever suits your style.

Looking Closer

Two Bible readings from different parts of the Bible, showing how the New Testament relates to and builds on the Old Testament, and how history, poetry, gospels and letters all link together.

Do feel free to read more than the short excerpts printed here. It's always a good idea to read the full passage in context.

Engaging

Some reflections to help us engage creatively with the ideas behind the text.

Talking and Listening

Take a few moments to settle into silence and use this short prayer as a prompt for a conversation with God.

The Big Story

Story

The Bible as a Connected Story
for
Lent and Holy Week

Week One

The Beginning of Everything

Ash Wednesday

At the start of the story, before the beginning of everything, there was the Word; and the Word was, and the Word was with, and the Word was speaking; and the Spirit of God was over the waters ...

Thursday

And the world waited in the dark and silence, hardly daring even to breathe; and God burst in and made light and land, trees and time, protons and planets and pencils; and God looked, and it was good ...

Friday

And God made people from the dust of the earth: women and men and girls and boys, to be with God, to reflect God's glory, to love and be loved by God, and to take care of the garden; and it was very, very good ...

Saturday

And the people walked with each other and with God in the garden, and they had all they needed, and God allowed the people to choose their destiny, whether they would follow God's ways or follow their own ...

Sunday

But the people chose to be masters of their own fate and did not follow God's ways, and they started to lie and blame and hurt each other, and they had to leave the garden where God walked in the cool of the day.

Perhaps they thought this was the end of the story.

But it was not.

1

1 Ash Wednesday

The Big Story

At the start of the story, before the beginning of everything, there was the Word; and the Word was, and the Word was with, and the Word was speaking; and the Spirit of God was over the waters …

What do you think it was like at the beginning of everything?

🔍 Looking Closer

John 1:1-5 (ERV)

Jesus
God   *Jesus*

Before the world began, the Word was there. The Word was
with God, and the Word was God. He was there with God in
the beginning.   *Jesus*   *Jesus*

Everything was made through him, and nothing was made
without him. In him there was life, and that life was a light for
the people of the world. The light shines in the darkness, and
the darkness has not defeated it.

Genesis 1:1-5 (GW)

In the beginning God created heaven and earth.

The earth was formless and empty, and darkness covered the
deep water. The Spirit of God was hovering over the water.

Then God said, "Let there be light!" So there was light. God saw
the light was good. So God separated the light from the
darkness. God named the light *day*, and the darkness he
named *night*. There was evening, then morning—the first day.

Engaging

I love the beginning of John's gospel. I'm not quite sure I know what it means, but I love it. It reflects the very start of the Bible, where nothing is, except God.

But somehow God is not alone. We read of the creative Word who both is God and is with God. And we see, hovering over the unformed void, God's spirit who works God's words, yet is God too.

The Bible shows us different aspects of God at different times. It's like a flock of birds, swooping and turning as one, ever-changing, yet ever the same. Sometimes a mighty ruler, sometimes a tender parent, sometimes personal and approachable, sometimes utterly other.

Eternal wisdom, logos, creative word, hovering spirit – It's all a bit beyond my grasp, but beautiful.

Talking and Listening

Eternal Father,
  Creative Word, *Jesus*
    Spirit-over-the-waters,

I find myself lost in wonder.

I don't pretend to understand
  how you existed before time,
    how you spoke all into being,
      how you came as a human yet fully God.

But the fact that I can't get my head round it
  does not make it less true.

It just means I find myself lost in wonder again.

Amen.

2   Thursday

The Big Story

... and the world waited in the dark and silence, hardly daring even to breathe; and God burst in and made light and land, trees and time, protons and planets and pencils; and God looked, and it was good ...

What do you think it would have been like, to see all things come into being?

Looking Closer

Genesis 1:20-21, 24-25 (NCV)

Then God said, "Let the water be filled with living things, and let birds fly in the air above the earth."

So God created the large sea animals and every living thing that moves in the sea. The sea is filled with these living things, with each one producing more of its own kind. He also made every bird that flies, and each bird produced more of its own kind. God saw that this was good.

Then God said, "Let the earth be filled with animals, each producing more of its own kind. Let there be tame animals and small crawling animals and wild animals, and let each produce more of its kind." And it happened.

So God made the wild animals, the tame animals, and all the small crawling animals to produce more of their own kind. God saw that this was good.

Matthew 10:29-31 (NIV)

Are not two sparrows sold for a penny? Yet not one of them will fall to the ground outside your Father's care. And even the very hairs of your head are all numbered. So don't be afraid; you are worth more than many sparrows.

Engaging

In the bird-watching world, sparrows are often called LBJs, Little Brown Jobs. In other words, one of the dozens of similar small, greyish brown species that rarely catch the attention and hardly anyone bothers to note.

Except God. Apparently, God is a keen 'twitcher' and has a very expansive notebook of LBJs. Come the time for nestlings to learn to fly I expect noting every crash landing keeps him rather busy.

And what about us? Does God note our crash landings?

Yes, we are gently assured. God even knows the hairs on your head, so every baby step of faith, every setback, every minor triumph, every struggle – all are seen, and noted, and cared about.

You are worth more than many sparrows.

Talking and Listening

Blessed are you, Lord our God,
   king of the universe,
for you created all things
and yet you see me.

Your greatness is displayed in the heavens
   and on the earth.
Your compassion is shown to all.

Praise be to your name for ever.

Amen.

3   Friday

The Big Story

... and God made people from the dust of the earth: women and men and girls and boys, to be with God, to reflect God's glory, to love and be loved by God, and to take care of the garden; and it was very, very good ...

You are made in God's image. How does that make you feel?

Looking Closer

Genesis 1:26-28, 31 (ERV)

Then God said, "Now let's make humans who will be like us. They will rule over all the fish in the sea and the birds in the air. They will rule over all the large animals and all the little things that crawl on the earth."

So God created humans in his own image. He created them to be like himself. He created them male and female. God blessed them and said to them, "Have many children. Fill the earth and take control of it. Rule over the fish in the sea and the birds in the air. Rule over every living thing that moves on the earth."

God looked at everything he had made. And he saw that everything was very good.

There was evening, and then there was morning. This was the sixth day.

Psalm 19:1-6 (NIV)

For the director of music. A psalm of David.
The heavens declare the glory of God;
    the skies proclaim the work of his hands.
Day after day they pour forth speech;
    night after night they reveal knowledge.
They have no speech, they use no words;
    no sound is heard from them.
Yet their voice goes out into all the earth,
    their words to the ends of the world.
In the heavens God has pitched a tent for the sun.
    It is like a bridegroom coming out of his chamber,
    like a champion rejoicing to run his course.
It rises at one end of the heavens
    and makes its circuit to the other;
    nothing is deprived of its warmth.

Engaging

All creation declares God's glory: worms by being wormy, pelicans by being pelican-y and humans by being ... not human-y, but Godly, for we are made in his image.

There's a reason that God has a bit of a downer on us making graven images, and that is because *God has already made his image* – and it's us! God has made people to be like him, to show his glory and reflect his nature.

It's quite amazing, I live next door to someone made in the image of God!

I'm not suggesting that you put your neighbour on a pedestal and pour out drink offerings, or anything, but, as C.S. Lewis puts it, "There are no ordinary people. You have never talked to a mere mortal."

Kind of puts things into perspective.

Talking and Listening

Dear Lord,

please help me this day
  to see your image in those around me,
    to see your glory reflected,
      however dimly.
Help me to see others as you do,
  to see their worth,
    and to see my worth, too.

Amen.

4 Saturday

The Big Story

... and the people walked with each other and with God in the garden, and they had all they needed, and God allowed the people to choose their destiny, whether they would follow God's ways or follow their own ...

Why do you think God allowed the people to choose?

Looking Closer

Genesis 2:8-9, 15-17 (NCV)

Then the Lord God planted a garden in the east, in a place called Eden, and put the man he had formed into it. The Lord God caused every beautiful tree and every tree that was good for food to grow out of the ground. In the middle of the garden, God put the tree that gives life and also the tree that gives the knowledge of good and evil.

The Lord God put the man in the garden of Eden to care for it and work it. The Lord God commanded him, "You may eat the fruit from any tree in the garden, but you must not eat the fruit from the tree which gives the knowledge of good and evil. If you ever eat fruit from that tree, you will die!"

Psalm 145:8-10, 15-16 (NRSV)

The Lord is gracious and merciful,
    slow to anger and abounding in steadfast love.
The Lord is good to all,
    and his compassion is over all that he has made.

All your works shall give thanks to you, O Lord,
    and all your faithful shall bless you.
The eyes of all look to you,
    and you give them their food in due season.
You open your hand,
    satisfying the desire of every living thing.

Engaging

This is a story about all of us. The Hebrew word *adam* here just means person, generic human. So this is all of us being given the choice:

How do we define right and wrong?

Is it what our parents taught us, or what our friends think, or the law of the land? Is morality determined by the accident of the time and place of our birth?

Some things, such as slavery, that are obviously wrong, were once perfectly acceptable. Other things that we now consider normal would have shocked our ancestors. So, is everything relative? Or is there such a thing as actual right and wrong?

The easy answer is that right and wrong are defined by God. *"The Bible says it, I believe it, that settles it"*, as some have put it. But perhaps that is a bit simplistic. Racial segregation was justified with the Bible, and Nazi Germany had the backing of the official church. So translating what God wants into what we think God wants is not as simple as it might be.

We read our Bibles through the lenses of culture, experience and assumptions. How can we tell when we are applying God's standards using our God-given judgement and when we are reading what we want to read?

Talking and Listening

God of Justice and Truth,

you created us with a sense of your divine goodness,
    so we know instinctively the wholesome savour of good,
        and the acrid stench of wrong.

Yet at times this sense becomes corrupted,
    and your people, made in your image,
        become a mangled, distorted caricature.

Forgive us when we silence the voice of righteousness,
    and put our own agendas before your word.
        Forgive us and help us.

Amen.

First Sunday in Lent

The Big Story

... but the people chose to be masters of their own fate and did not follow God's ways, and they started to lie and blame and hurt each other, and they had to leave the garden where God walked in the cool of the day.

Perhaps they thought this was the end of the story.
But it was not.

What do you think the people felt as they left the garden?

🔍 Looking Closer

Genesis 3:6-13, 22-24 (MSG)

When the Woman saw that the tree looked like good eating and realized what she would get out of it—she'd know everything!—she took and ate the fruit and then gave some to her husband, and he ate.

Immediately the two of them did "see what's really going on"—saw themselves naked! They sewed fig leaves together as makeshift clothes for themselves. When they heard the sound of God strolling in the garden in the evening breeze, the Man and his Wife hid in the trees of the garden, hid from God.

God called to the Man: "Where are you?" He said, "I heard you in the garden and I was afraid because I was naked. And I hid."

God said, "Who told you you were naked? Did you eat from that tree I told you not to eat from?" The Man said, "The Woman you gave me as a companion, she gave me fruit from the tree, and, yes, I ate it."

God said to the Woman, "What is this that you've done?" "The serpent seduced me", she said, "and I ate."

God said, "The Man has become like one of us, capable of knowing everything, ranging from good to evil. What if he now should reach out and take fruit from the Tree-of-Life and eat, and live forever? Never—this cannot happen!"

So God expelled them from the Garden of Eden and sent them to work the ground, the same dirt out of which they'd been made. He threw them out of the garden and stationed angel-cherubim and a revolving sword of fire east of it, guarding the path to the Tree-of-Life.

Deuteronomy 30:11-14, 19 (NCV)

This command I give you today is not too hard for you; it is not beyond what you can do. It is not up in heaven. You do not have to ask, "Who will go up to heaven and get it for us so we can obey it and keep it?" It is not on the other side of the sea. You do not have to ask, "Who will go across the sea and get it? Who will tell it to us so we can keep it?" No, the word is very near you. It is in your mouth and in your heart so you may obey it.

Today I ask heaven and earth to be witnesses. I am offering you life or death, blessings or curses. Now, choose life!

Engaging

This is one of the saddest sentences in the Bible. *They heard the sound of God strolling in the garden … and they hid.*

They knew they'd messed up – big time – but they didn't know God and his gracious nature.

God sought them out, and sorted them out, then sent them out to safety. They had chosen to define right and wrong for themselves, and spoiled God's perfect world. God could not allow them to enter eternal life in their state of disgrace, so the banishment was protection, not penalty.

Time after time, across the millennia, God offers and reoffers humanity the choice: Come walk with me in my garden in the cool of the day, or choose to live without me – no rules, but no hope – outside the garden.

Life or death, blessings or curses. Please, choose life!

Talking and Listening

Loving Father,

You are gracious and compassionate,
    slow to anger and rich in love.
You are good to all;
    and have compassion on all you have made.

Have mercy on us.

Amen.

Week Two

From Promise to Slavery

Monday

And generations passed, and God called Abraham and Sarah to go to the land that God would show them, and God promised that their children would be as the stars in the sky, as the sand on the shore; and Abraham believed, and it was credited to him as righteousness ...

Tuesday

And God made a covenant with Abraham and his offspring saying "I shall be your God and you shall be my people"; and God appeared to Abraham as three visitors, and Abraham walked with them in the cool of the day, and God was gracious to Sarah and she bore a son to Abraham in his old age, and they named him Isaac ...

Wednesday

And on Mount Moriah Abraham offered a sacrifice of his son, his only son whom he loved; and God would not be worshipped according to the customs of the land, and God stopped Abraham's hand, and God himself provided a lamb in place of the son ...

Thursday

And Isaac's son was Jacob, and Jacob dreamed of a ladder reaching to heaven and said, "God is here, and I did not know it"; and Jacob wrestled with God and asked, "Who are you?", and God replied, "Why do you ask?"; and God gave him the name Israel ...

Friday

And Israel gave his son Joseph a sumptuous coat, and Joseph's brothers were jealous and sold him into slavery in Egypt; and God raised Joseph to become second only to Pharaoh and gave Joseph the meaning of Pharaoh's dreams; and Joseph stored up grain ...

Saturday

And there was famine, and Joseph's brothers came to Egypt for food, and Joseph said, "You meant it for harm, but God meant it for good", and Israel's children lived in Egypt, and had children, who had children, who had children; and they became a great nation, the children of the promise ...

Sunday

But there came a new king who did not know Joseph or Joseph's God, and he kept the children of Israel as slaves in Egypt, far from the land God had promised to Abraham, Isaac and Jacob; and their lives were bitter with hard labour.

Perhaps they thought this was the end of the story.

But it was not.

5   Monday

The Big Story

... and generations passed, and God called Abraham and Sarah to go to the land that God would show them, and God promised that their children would be as the stars in the sky, as the sand on the shore; and Abraham believed, and it was credited to him as righteousness ...

If you were Abraham, how would you feel about this promise?

Looking Closer

Genesis 15:1-6 (NIV)

After this, the word of the Lord came to Abram in a vision:

"Do not be afraid, Abram.
  I am your shield,
  your very great reward."

But Abram said, "Sovereign Lord, what can you give me since I remain childless and the one who will inherit my estate is Eliezer of Damascus?" And Abram said, "You have given me no children; so a servant in my household will be my heir."

Then the word of the Lord came to him: "This man will not be your heir, but a son who is your own flesh and blood will be your heir." He took him outside and said, "Look up at the sky and count the stars—if indeed you can count them." Then he said to him, "So shall your offspring be."

Abram believed the Lord, and he credited it to him as righteousness.

Romans 4:1-8 (WEB)

What then will we say that Abraham, our forefather, has found according to the flesh? For if Abraham was justified by works, he has something to boast about, but not toward God. For what does the Scripture say? "Abraham believed God, and it was accounted to him for righteousness."

Now to him who works, the reward is not counted as grace, but as something owed. But to him who doesn't work, but believes in him who justifies the ungodly, his faith is accounted for righteousness. Even as David also pronounces blessing on the man to whom God counts righteousness apart from works, "Blessed are they whose iniquities are forgiven, whose sins are covered. Blessed is the man whom the Lord will by no means charge with sin."

Engaging

We skip forward a few generations from Adam to Abraham (Abram as he was then), and meet a man with remarkable trust, even in the face of impossible odds.

You get what you pay for, modern wisdom tells us. *There is no such thing as a free lunch.* And despite the scam emails telling us we are the fortunate recipients of a cash windfall, *if it looks too good to be true, it probably is.*

But God's kingdom is upside down. Here, you *do* get something for nothing, it seems.

Abraham had not actually *done* anything righteous, but God chalked it up to his account as if he had. It's like not turning up for the first day of your new job, but being paid anyway, or not sitting the exam, but passing anyway.

Jesus told a story about this in Matthew 20. The workers who turned up right at the end of the day were paid the same as those who had worked since daybreak. Some complained that this was not fair. "Can't I do what I want with my own money?" replied the owner. "Is it a problem if I'm generous?"

Yes, God's kingdom is upside down. Or do I mean ours?

Talking and Listening

God of Unreasonable Grace,

You are far more generous than you need be.
   You are far more merciful than anyone could expect.
      You believe in me far more than I think sensible
         You love me far more than I can possibly imagine.

Thank you for your unreasonable grace

Amen.

6   Tuesday

The Big Story

… and God made a covenant with Abraham and his offspring saying "I shall be your God and you shall be my people"; and God appeared to Abraham as three visitors, and Abraham walked with them in the cool of the day, and God was gracious to Sarah and she bore a son to Abraham in his old age, and they named him Isaac …

These three visitors are often seen as an early appearance of the Trinity. How do you think God might appear today?

🔍 Looking Closer

Genesis 18:1-5, 9-10a, 16-19 (NCV)

Later, the Lord again appeared to Abraham near the great trees of Mamre. Abraham was sitting at the entrance of his tent … He looked up and saw three men standing near him. When Abraham saw them, he ran from his tent to meet them. He bowed facedown on the ground before them and said, "Sir, if you think well of me, please stay awhile with me, your servant. I will bring some water so all of you can wash your feet. You may rest under the tree, and I will get some bread for you so you can regain your strength. Then you may continue your journey." The three men said, "That is fine. Do as you said."

The men asked Abraham, "Where is your wife Sarah?" "There, in the tent", said Abraham. Then the Lord said, "I will certainly return to you about this time a year from now. At that time your wife Sarah will have a son." Then the men got up to leave and started out toward Sodom. Abraham walked along with them a short time to send them on their way.

The Lord said, "Should I tell Abraham what I am going to do now? Abraham's children will certainly become a great and powerful nation, and all nations on earth will be blessed through him. I have chosen him so he would command his children and his descendants to live the way the Lord wants them to, to live right and be fair. Then I, the Lord, will give Abraham what I promised him."

Hebrews 11:8-12 (NIV)

By faith Abraham, when called to go to a place he would later receive as his inheritance, obeyed and went, even though he did not know where he was going.

By faith he made his home in the promised land like a stranger in a foreign country; he lived in tents, as did Isaac and Jacob, who were heirs with him of the same promise. For he was looking forward to the city with foundations, whose architect and builder is God.

And by faith even Sarah, who was past childbearing age, was enabled to bear children because she considered him faithful who had made the promise. And so from this one man, and he as good as dead, came descendants as numerous as the stars in the sky and as countless as the sand on the seashore.

Engaging

These passages contain two of my favourite pictures. The first is an actual picture. It shows the enigmatic visitors with symbols of the three persons of the Trinity.

Strikingly, the table has an empty space at the front, as if they are waiting for someone to join them. Are they waiting for me?

The second picture is the hauntingly beautiful phrase that Abraham was "waiting for the eternal city that God had planned and built".

Something better than the Promised Land? I wonder what that might be.

Talking and Listening

God of Abraham,

May we, too, hold lightly onto this world's blessings.
May we see ourselves as citizens of heaven,
    and sojourners on earth,
as we wait to take our place at your table.

Amen.

7   Wednesday

The Big Story

… and on Mount Moriah Abraham offered a sacrifice of his son, his only son whom he loved; and God would not be worshipped according to the customs of the land, and God stopped Abraham's hand, and God himself provided a lamb in place of the son …

What do you think was going on here?

🔍 Looking Closer

Genesis 22:1-13 (MSG)

After all this, God tested Abraham. God said, "Abraham!" "Yes?" answered Abraham. "I'm listening." He said, "Take your dear son Isaac whom you love and go to the land of Moriah. Sacrifice him there as a burnt offering on one of the mountains that I'll point out to you."

Abraham got up early in the morning and saddled his donkey. He took two of his young servants and his son Isaac. He had split wood for the burnt offering. He set out for the place God had directed him. On the third day he looked up and saw the place in the distance. Abraham told his two young servants, "Stay here with the donkey. The boy and I are going over there to worship; then we'll come back to you."

Abraham took the wood for the burnt offering and gave it to Isaac his son to carry. He carried the flint and the knife. The two of them went off together.

Isaac said to Abraham his father, "Father?" "Yes, my son." "We have flint and wood, but where's the sheep for the burnt offering?" Abraham said, "Son, God will see to it that there's a sheep for the burnt offering." And they kept on walking together.

They arrived at the place to which God had directed him. Abraham built an altar. He laid out the wood. Then he tied up Isaac and laid him on the wood. Abraham reached out and took the knife to kill his son.

Just then an angel of God called to him out of Heaven, "Abraham! Abraham!" "Yes, I'm listening." "Don't lay a hand on that boy! Don't touch him! Now I know how fearlessly you fear God; you didn't hesitate to place your son, your dear son, on the altar for me."

Abraham looked up. He saw a ram caught by its horns in the thicket. Abraham took the ram and sacrificed it as a burnt offering instead of his son.

Deuteronomy 12:29-31 (NCV)

You will enter the land and take it away from the nations that the Lord your God will destroy ahead of you. When you force them out and live in their land, they will be destroyed for you, but be careful not to be trapped by asking about their gods.

Don't say, "How do these nations worship? I will do the same." Don't worship the Lord your God that way, because the Lord hates the evil ways they worship their gods. They even burn their sons and daughters as sacrifices to their gods!

Engaging

What a dreadful story! I'd be much happier if this were not in the Bible. But its inclusion assures me that Scripture is not just invented, or stories for kiddies (who would make this up?), and that we don't have to avoid difficult questions.

It is so appalling to us because we are reading it with 21ˢᵗ century eyes. In Abraham and Isaac's world, sacrificing a child was how some people worshipped their gods, but the point of this story is *definitely not* that God wants Abraham to kill his son. Nor that God is playing some nasty mind trick. Notice what Abraham says to his servants: *The boy and I are going over there to worship; then we'll come back to you.* We'll come back. Both of us. Abraham expected Isaac to return. Maybe he didn't know how, but he trusted God.

And God is making a point. *Other people might worship their gods in this way, but do you really think I'm like that?*

Talking and Listening

Righteous Lord,

We confess the weakness of our understanding,
 and the smallness of our vision of you.
We continually make you in our image,
 and project our own faults onto you.

We make you out to be a tyrant,
 when your law is for our life and protection.
We cast you as cruel,
 when your justice is all goodness and mercy.
We remember your anger
 and forget your compassion.

Forgive us for our lack of trust,
 and help us to see you as you are,
  not how we fear you might be.

Amen.

8   Thursday

The Big Story

... and Isaac's son was Jacob, and Jacob dreamed of a ladder reaching to heaven and said, "God is here, and I did not know it"; and Jacob wrestled with God and asked, "Who are you?", and God replied, "Why do you ask?"; and God gave him the name Israel ...

What name might God give to you?

🔍 Looking Closer

Genesis 32: 24-30 (MSG)

But Jacob stayed behind by himself, and a man wrestled with him until daybreak. When the man saw that he couldn't get the best of Jacob as they wrestled, he deliberately threw Jacob's hip out of joint.

The man said, "Let me go; it's daybreak." Jacob said, "I'm not letting you go 'til you bless me."

The man said, "What's your name?" He answered, "Jacob." The man said, "But no longer. Your name is no longer Jacob. From now on it's Israel (God-Wrestler); you've wrestled with God and you've come through."

Jacob asked, "And what's your name?" The man said, "Why do you want to know my name?" And then, right then and there, he blessed him.

Jacob named the place Peniel (God's Face) because, he said, "I saw God face-to-face and lived to tell the story!"

Matthew 8:5-11 (NIV)

When Jesus had entered Capernaum, a centurion came to him, asking for help. "Lord", he said, "my servant lies at home paralyzed, suffering terribly."

Jesus said to him, "Shall I come and heal him?" The centurion replied, "Lord, I do not deserve to have you come under my roof. But just say the word, and my servant will be healed. For I myself am a man under authority, with soldiers under me. I tell this one, 'Go,' and he goes; and that one, 'Come,' and he comes. I say to my servant, 'Do this,' and he does it."

When Jesus heard this, he was amazed and said to those following him, "Truly I tell you, I have not found anyone in Israel with such great faith. I say to you that many will come from the east and the west, and will take their places at the feast with Abraham, Isaac and Jacob in the kingdom of heaven."

Engaging

Names are funny things. Mine means 'fairy', but I have yet to sprout wings or transform a pumpkin.

Jacob's name means 'deceiver', and it suited him well. He was a sneaky, conniving cheat. Yet we find him listed by Jesus as feasting in the kingdom of heaven.

Abraham, Isaac and Jacob – the three great men of the faith.

Or were they? To be honest, if I were to be naming a set of patriarchs to define my people, I'd have stopped at Isaac. Jacob is a bit of an embarrassment. Mind you, Abraham wasn't perfect, and Isaac had his moments too.

Let's face it, none of us are part of God's kingdom because we've earned our citizenship though some points system – 10 points for being a Sunday school teacher (shortage subject), 20 points for having relatives in the country …

Fortunately for us, God has a very inclusive visa system.

Talking and Listening

Eternal King,

Thank you that your kingdom has room enough
  for all kinds of strangers.
Thank you that you welcome waifs and strays
  to eat with you at the banquet table of heaven.
Thank you that there is no-one so far away
  that they might not be brought near, by your grace.

Amen.

9 Friday

The Big Story

... and Israel gave his son Joseph a sumptuous coat, and Joseph's brothers were jealous and sold him into slavery in Egypt; and God raised Joseph to become second only to Pharaoh and gave Joseph the meaning of Pharaoh's dreams; and Joseph stored up grain ...

How do you think Joseph felt while he was a slave in Egypt?

Looking Closer

Genesis 41:15-16, 25, 39-40 (ERV)

Pharaoh said to Joseph, "I had a dream, and no one can explain it for me. I heard that you can explain dreams when someone tells you about them."

Joseph answered, "I cannot! But God can explain the dream for you, Pharaoh."

Then Joseph said to Pharaoh, "Both of these dreams have the same meaning. God is telling you what will happen soon."

So Pharaoh said to Joseph, "God showed these things to you, so you must be the wisest man. I will put you in charge of my country, and the people will obey all your commands. I will be the only one more powerful than you."

Isaiah 43:1b-7 (GW)

Do not be afraid, because I have reclaimed you.
    I have called you by name; you are mine.
When you go through the sea, I am with you.
When you go through rivers, they will not sweep you away.
When you walk through fire, you will not be burned,
    and the flames will not harm you.

I am the Lord your God, the Holy One of Israel, your Saviour.
    Egypt is the ransom I exchanged for you.
    Sudan and Seba are the price I paid for you.
Since you are precious to me,
    you are honoured and I love you.
I will exchange others for you.
    Nations will be the price I pay for your life.

Do not be afraid, because I am with you.
    I will bring your descendants from the east
        and gather you from the west.
I will say to the north, "Give them up",
    and to the south, "Do not keep them".
Bring my sons from far away

and my daughters from the ends of the earth.
Bring everyone who is called by my name,
   whom I created for my glory,
   whom I formed and made.

Engaging

Today's part of The Big Story summarises a solid 12 chapters. That's over 1% of the whole Bible just for one guy!

It's a real roller-coaster of a life: highs, then lows, then deeper lows then soaring highs. Honestly, someone should write a musical about it. Oh, wait …

But as we read the story, we see the end from the beginning. We read about Joseph sold into slavery, Joseph unfairly imprisoned, Joseph forgotten and left to rot, and we know it will all come out right in the end. Joseph didn't.

The only thing that Joseph could do as he spent year after bleak year waiting for … something, anything … was to hold on to the God he trusted. *I am with you. When you go through the sea, I am with you.*

Talking and Listening

Faithful God,

Sometimes I pass through deep waters
   and it seems as though the tides will sweep me away.

I cannot hear your voice for the crash of waves.
   I cannot feel your presence for the smack of surf.
     I cannot see your light while my eyes are blinded with salt.

The tangling seaweed pulls me down.
   The chilling waters numb my bones.
     Yet you are there. You are with me. You redeem me.

Thanks be to your name for ever.

Amen.

10 Saturday

The Big Story

… and there was famine, and Joseph's brothers came to Egypt for food, and Joseph said, "You meant it for harm, but God meant it for good", and Israel's children lived in Egypt, and had children, who had children, who had children; and they became a great nation, the children of the promise …

God's promise to Abraham took a long time to come true. What are you waiting for?

🔍 Looking Closer

Genesis 50:19-20, 24-26 (NIV)

But Joseph said to them, "Don't be afraid. Am I in the place of God? You intended to harm me, but God intended it for good to accomplish what is now being done, the saving of many lives."

Then Joseph said to his brothers, "I am about to die. But God will surely come to your aid and take you up out of this land to the land he promised on oath to Abraham, Isaac and Jacob."

And Joseph made the Israelites swear an oath and said, "God will surely come to your aid, and then you must carry my bones up from this place."

So Joseph died at the age of a hundred and ten. And after they embalmed him, he was placed in a coffin in Egypt.

Romans 9:6-8 (ERV)

I don't mean that God failed to keep his promise to the Jewish people. But only some of the people of Israel are really God's people. And only some of Abraham's descendants are true children of Abraham.

This is what God said to Abraham: "Your true descendants will be those who come through Isaac." This means that not all of Abraham's descendants are God's true children. Abraham's true children are those who become God's children because of the promise he made to Abraham.

🧠 Engaging

If I'm honest, I have no idea what's going on a lot of the time. I don't just mean with God-stuff. I don't know what's going in in my children's heads most days, and I even flummox myself occasionally. "Why on earth did I do *that*?"

So it's not surprising that God's ways are sometimes a mystery to me. *"You meant it for harm, but God meant it for good",* said *Joseph.* Huh? I'm sure it'll all become clear on the far side of glory. (I expect it'll take the whole of eternity to go round saying, "Oh, so *that's* why that happened. I get it now!")

One thing that has puzzled me is 'the children of Abraham'. He had quite a few, you know, not just Isaac and Ishmael. But only the descendants of Isaac count. And only Isaac's son Jacob. What about all the other children of Abraham?

But it was never about blood-lines and ancestors. God's family is made of adopted children. Paul explains it well:

> "It is not the children by physical descent who are God's children, but it is the children of the promise who are regarded as Abraham's offspring."

Phew. At least that's one thing off the "Oh, *now* I get it!" list.

Talking and Listening

Loving Father,

You see the whole of time and eternity,
  as if set out on a tapestry.
You know how all things will come to be,
  while we see only our small part of time and space.

Thank you that we can trust you
  to place every stich perfectly.
Help us to work with you
  even though all we see
    are the tangled threads
      at the back of the work.

Amen.

Second Sunday in Lent

The Big Story

... but there came a new king who did not know Joseph or Joseph's God, and he kept the children of Israel as slaves in Egypt, far from the land God had promised to Abraham, Isaac and Jacob; and their lives were bitter with hard labour.

Perhaps they thought this was the end of the story.
But it was not.

How do you cope when promises seem to fail?

🔍 Looking Closer

Exodus 1:8-14 (GW)

Then a new king, who knew nothing about Joseph, began to rule in Egypt. He said to his people, "There are too many Israelites, and they are stronger than we are. We have to outsmart them, or they'll increase in number. Then, if war breaks out, they will join our enemies, fight against us, and leave the country."

So the Egyptians put slave drivers in charge of them in order to oppress them through forced labour. They built Pithom and Rameses as supply cities for Pharaoh. But the more the Israelites were oppressed, the more they increased in number and spread out.

The Egyptians couldn't stand them any longer. So they forced the Israelites to work hard as slaves. They made their lives bitter with back-breaking work in mortar and bricks and every kind of work in the fields. All the jobs the Egyptians gave them were brutally hard.

John 8:31-36 (NIV)

To the Jews who had believed him, Jesus said, "If you hold to my teaching, you are really my disciples. Then you will know the truth, and the truth will set you free."

They answered him, "We are Abraham's descendants and have never been slaves of anyone. How can you say that we shall be set free?"

Jesus replied, "Very truly I tell you, everyone who sins is a slave to sin. Now a slave has no permanent place in the family, but a son belongs to it forever. So if the Son sets you free, you will be free indeed."

Engaging

It is very interesting that when Jesus offered freedom to some of his fellow-Jews, they indignantly replied that as Abraham's children they had never been slaves of anyone.

Had they forgotten that delightful vacation in Egypt? Or the extended holiday in Babylon? Or the fact that they were a vassal state of the mighty Roman Empire at that very moment?

Why did they make such an obviously false statement?

I suspect it was an early case of foot-in-mouth disease. They were offended that Jesus had said they needed setting free and that he was the person to do it, and they put tongue in gear before engaging brain. "*How dare he?*", they fumed, "*We're good Jews and we don't need the likes of him to 'fix' us. We don't need fixing, thank you very much!*"

But people can be slaves without knowing it. Paul puts it like this: "*Surely you know that when you give yourselves like slaves to obey someone, then you are really slaves of that person. The person you obey is your master. You can follow sin, which brings spiritual death, or you can obey God, which makes you right with him.*" (Romans 6:16 NCV)

Talking and Listening

Lord God,

Grant us the wisdom to discern the chains that we wear:
   chains that bind us and hold us down,
     chains that keep us from following you,
      chains that bow our heads into darkness.

We offer these chains to you.
   Please break them, shatter them, destroy them,
     and in their place forge links of life
      so that we may be ever be bound to you.

Amen.

Week Three

From Slavery to Promise

Monday

And God sent a baby, born to a peasant woman and hidden in a basket, to rescue the people from their slavery; and Pharaoh's daughter drew him from the river and named him Moses; and the boy grew to manhood in Pharaoh's palace and killed an Egyptian slave master, and ran to the wilderness in fear and lived as a shepherd for forty years ...

Tuesday

And Moses came to the mountain of God and there saw a bush that was burning yet did not burn, and God called Moses and Moses asked, "Who are you?", and God replied, "I am being who I am being, I am who is, I am who was, I am who is to come" ...

Wednesday

And the people groaned in the anguish of their slavery, and God heard them and did not forget the covenant with Abraham, Isaac and Jacob; and God spoke to the people saying, "I will have you as my own people and you will have me as your God"; and God spoke to Pharaoh saying, "Let my people go!" ...

Thursday

And Pharaoh's heart was hard and he did not let God's people go; and God sent plagues from the water and from the sky, plagues of sickness and of hunger; and there was darkness for three days, and still Pharaoh's heart was hard; and there was a final plague: the death of the firstborn ...

41

Friday

And God told the people to take a perfect lamb for a sacrifice, and put its blood on the cross posts of their houses, and the people obeyed and waited in silence, hardly daring even to breathe, as they looked for God's deliverance ...

Saturday

And that night the firstborn died, and God's people sheltered beneath the blood of the lamb that was slain, and God brooded over them and did not permit the destroyer to enter their houses, and God's people left Egypt that very night ...

Sunday

But the people came to the waters of the Red Sea and they could not cross, and they heard the horses and chariots of the Egyptians thundering in the distance; and they cried out against Moses saying, "Were there no graves for us in Egypt?"

Perhaps they thought this was the end of the story.

But it was not.

11 Monday

The Big Story

... and God sent a baby, born to a peasant woman and hidden in a basket, to rescue the people from their slavery; and Pharaoh's daughter drew him from the river and named him Moses; and the boy grew to manhood in Pharaoh's palace and killed an Egyptian slave master, and ran to the wilderness in fear and lived as a shepherd for forty years ...

What do you think of Moses' CV?

🔍 Looking Closer

Exodus 2:1-3, 5-7, 10 (NRSV)

Now a man from the house of Levi went and married a Levite woman. The woman conceived and bore a son; and when she saw that he was a fine baby, she hid him three months. When she could hide him no longer she got a papyrus basket for him, and plastered it with bitumen and pitch; she put the child in it and placed it among the reeds on the bank of the river.

The daughter of Pharaoh came down to bathe at the river, while her attendants walked beside the river. She saw the basket among the reeds and sent her maid to bring it. When she opened it, she saw the child. He was crying, and she took pity on him. "This must be one of the Hebrews' children", she said. Then his sister said to Pharaoh's daughter, "Shall I go and get you a nurse from the Hebrew women to nurse the child for you?"

When the child grew up, she brought him to Pharaoh's daughter, and she took him as her son. She named him Moses, "because", she said, "I drew him out of the water."

Acts 7:17-19, 21-24, 26-29 (NIV)

As the time drew near for God to fulfil his promise to Abraham, the number of our people in Egypt had greatly increased. Then 'a new king, to whom Joseph meant nothing, came to power in Egypt.' He dealt treacherously with our people and oppressed our ancestors by forcing them to throw out their newborn babies so that they would die.

When he was placed outside, Pharaoh's daughter took him and brought him up as her own son. Moses was educated in all the wisdom of the Egyptians and was powerful in speech and action.

When Moses was forty years old, he decided to visit his own people, the Israelites. He saw one of them being mistreated by an Egyptian, so he went to his defence and avenged him by killing the Egyptian. The next day Moses came upon two Israelites who were fighting. He tried to reconcile them by saying, "Men, you are brothers; why do you want to hurt each other?"

But the man who was mistreating the other pushed Moses aside and said, "Who made you ruler and judge over us? Are you thinking of killing me as you killed the Egyptian yesterday?" When Moses heard this, he fled to Midian, where he settled as a foreigner and had two sons.

Engaging

Imagine, a Cambridge graduate, rising political star, visits his home town and sees workers being exploited. Time for the local hero! He organises a protest march, but it turns nasty. There is fighting, he finds blood on his hands and suddenly he's a wanted man. He flees the country and finds work as a road sweeper in Nowheresville. How the mighty have fallen.

At forty, Moses should have been at the peak of his power – why else had he spent all those years of study? Moses was trained as diplomat, a cabinet minister, a prince of the world's superpower. He should have been leading men, not sheep. And they weren't even his own sheep. What a waste of a life.

But not from God's point of view.

Talking and Listening

God of all wisdom,

It can be hard to follow your path,
  when we can see our own way forward.
May we learn to have confidence in you
  when we think we know better,
and trust you with our whole hearts
  instead of leaning on our own understanding.

Amen.

12 Tuesday

The Big Story

... and Moses came to the mountain of God and there saw a bush that was burning yet did not burn, and God called Moses and Moses asked, "Who are you?", and God replied, "I am being who I am being, I am who is, I am who was, I am who is to come" ...

What do you think God's reply means?

Looking Closer

Exodus 3:1-6, 9-10, 13-14 (MSG)

Moses was shepherding the flock of Jethro, his father-in-law, the priest of Midian. He led the flock to the west end of the wilderness and came to the mountain of God, Horeb. The angel of God appeared to him in flames of fire blazing out of the middle of a bush. He looked. The bush was blazing away but it didn't burn up. Moses said, "What's going on here? I can't believe this! Amazing! Why doesn't the bush burn up?"

God saw that he had stopped to look. God called to him from out of the bush, "Moses! Moses!" He said, "Yes? I'm right here!" God said, "Don't come any closer. Remove your sandals from your feet. You're standing on holy ground."

Then he said, "I am the God of your father: The God of Abraham, the God of Isaac, the God of Jacob." Moses hid his face, afraid to look at God. "The Israelite cry for help has come to me, and I've seen for myself how cruelly they're being treated by the Egyptians. It's time for you to go back: I'm sending you to Pharaoh to bring my people, the People of Israel, out of Egypt."

Then Moses said to God, "Suppose I go to the People of Israel and I tell them, 'The God of your fathers sent me to you'; and they ask me, 'What is his name?' What do I tell them?"

God said to Moses, "I-AM-WHO-I-AM. Tell the People of Israel, 'I-AM sent me to you.'"

Revelation 1:8, 12-18 (NIV)

"I am the Alpha and the Omega", says the Lord God, "who is, and who was, and who is to come, the Almighty."

I turned around to see the voice that was speaking to me. And when I turned I saw seven golden lampstands, and among the lampstands was someone like a son of man, dressed in a robe reaching down to his feet and with a golden sash around his chest. The hair on his head was white like wool, as white as snow, and his eyes were like blazing fire. His feet were like bronze glowing in a furnace, and his voice was like the sound of rushing waters. In his right hand he held seven stars, and coming out of his mouth was a sharp, double-edged sword. His face was like the sun shining in all its brilliance.

When I saw him, I fell at his feet as though dead. Then he placed his right hand on me and said: "Do not be afraid. I am the First and the Last. I am the Living One; I was dead, and now look, I am alive for ever and ever! And I hold the keys of death and Hades."

Engaging

It's a bit enigmatic isn't it? *I am who I am*. What kind of a name is that? And it's not even as straight forward as *I am who I am*. The Hebrew words could mean *I am what I am*, or *I will be who I will be*, or even *I cause to be what I cause to be*.

The problem is, how do you describe God? What larger concept would you use to define the infinite? What box could contain the supreme being? *I am me. That's all you need to know.*

Talking and Listening

All-surpassing God,

You exceed what our language can describe.
  You overwhelm what our imaginations can picture.
    You go beyond what our minds can comprehend.

Yet you make yourself know to your humble servants.
  You reveal yourself and your ways
    and became like us,
      so that we might be like you.

Praise be to your name for ever.

Amen.

13 Wednesday

The Big Story

… and the people groaned in the anguish of their slavery, and God heard them and did not forget the covenant with Abraham, Isaac and Jacob; and God spoke to the people saying, "I will have you as my own people and you will have me as your God"; and God spoke to Pharaoh saying, "Let my people go!" …

How would you cry out to God?

Looking Closer

Exodus 6:1-7 (GW)

Then the Lord said to Moses, "Now you will see what I will do to Pharaoh. I will show him my power, and he will let my people go. I will show him my power, and he will throw them out of his country."

God spoke to Moses, "I am the Lord. I appeared to Abraham, Isaac, and Jacob as God Almighty, but I didn't make myself known to them by my name, the Lord. I even made a promise to give them Canaan, the land where they lived as foreigners. Now I have heard the groaning of the Israelites, whom the Egyptians hold in slavery, and I have remembered my promise.

"Tell the Israelites, 'I am the Lord. I will bring you out from under the oppression of the Egyptians, and I will free you from slavery. I will rescue you with my powerful arm and with mighty acts of judgment. Then I will make you my people, and I will be your God. You will know that I am the Lord your God, who brought you out from under the forced labour of the Egyptians.'"

Psalm 102:1-2, 18-20 (MSG)

A prayer of one whose life is falling to pieces, and who lets God know just how bad it is

God, listen! Listen to my prayer,
　　listen to the pain in my cries.
Don't turn your back on me
　　just when I need you so desperately.
Pay attention! This is a cry for help!
　　And hurry—this can't wait!

Write this down for the next generation
　　so people not yet born will praise God:
"God looked out from his high holy place;
　　from heaven he surveyed the earth.
He listened to the groans of the doomed,
　　he opened the doors of their death cells."

Engaging

Times change. People don't.

Languages, forms of currency and styles of clothing vary across the years and miles. Being a human is the same as ever it was.

The psalm was written by David, hundreds of years after Moses, yet the thoughts are the same.

Today, in our very different culture, with our tech, our vast communication networks and our apparent sophistication, we are still the same people as cried out to the Lord in the Old Testament.

We still ask, *"Why me?"* We still struggle under dark clouds and cry out to the blank silence. We still want to know that someone notices what we're going through and that someone gives a damn.

Talking and Listening

Hear, O Lord, when I cry aloud,
    be gracious to me and answer me!
"Come", my heart says, "seek his face!"
    Your face, Lord, do I seek.
    Do not hide your face from me.

Do not turn your servant away in anger,
    you who have been my help.
Do not cast me off, do not forsake me,
    O God of my salvation!

Amen.

(Psalm 27:7-9 NRSV)

14 Thursday

The Big Story

... and Pharaoh's heart was hard and he did not let God's people go; and God sent plagues from the water and from the sky, plagues of sickness and of hunger; and there was darkness for three days, and still Pharaoh's heart was hard; and there was a final plague: the death of the firstborn ...

Why do you think God sent the plagues?

🔍 Looking Closer

Exodus 10:3, 21-23, 27-28 (NIV)

So Moses and Aaron went to Pharaoh and said to him, "This is what the Lord, the God of the Hebrews, says: 'How long will you refuse to humble yourself before me? Let my people go, so that they may worship me.'"

Then the Lord said to Moses, "Stretch out your hand toward the sky so that darkness spreads over Egypt—darkness that can be felt." So Moses stretched out his hand toward the sky, and total darkness covered all Egypt for three days. No one could see anyone else or move about for three days. Yet all the Israelites had light in the places where they lived.

But the Lord hardened Pharaoh's heart, and he was not willing to let them go. Pharaoh said to Moses, "Get out of my sight! Make sure you do not appear before me again! The day you see my face you will die."

Mark 15:33-39 (ERV)

At noon the whole country became dark. This darkness continued until three o'clock. At three o'clock Jesus cried out loudly, "*Eloi, Eloi, lama sabachthani.*" This means "My God, my God, why have you left me alone?"

Some of the people standing there heard this. They said, "Listen! He is calling Elijah."

One man there ran and got a sponge. He filled the sponge with sour wine and tied it to a stick. Then he used the stick to give the sponge to Jesus to get a drink from it. The man said, "We should wait now and see if Elijah will come to take him down from the cross."

Then Jesus cried out loudly and died.

When Jesus died, the curtain in the Temple was torn into two pieces. The tear started at the top and tore all the way to the bottom. The army officer who was standing there in front of the cross saw what happened when Jesus died. The officer said, "This man really was the Son of God!"

Engaging

Darkness. Sometimes it's literal, sometimes it's figurative. A lot of the time it's both.

Think of some the places where darkness is mentioned in the Bible. Biblical writers are often quite sparse on detail, so when they mention something, it's usually significant.

At the beginning of everything, darkness covered the void. Moses brought the people out of the darkness of Egypt and God spoke the law to them with a voice from the darkness.

It was night when the angels
   announced the coming saviour.
It was night when Nicodemus heard
   that God so loved the world.
It was night when Jesus was betrayed,
   and darkness fell as he died

And three days later it was still dark.

But then the light broke out.

Talking and Listening

Blessed are you, Lord our God,
   king of the universe,
for you have called us out of darkness
   into your marvellous light,
     and in your light, we see light.
Blessed be your name for ever.

Amen.

15 Friday

The Big Story

... and God told the people to take a perfect lamb for a sacrifice, and put its blood on the cross posts of their houses, and the people obeyed and waited in silence, hardly daring even to breathe, as they looked for God's deliverance ...

What does the slain, perfect lamb mean?

🔍 Looking Closer

Exodus 12:21-28 (NCV)

Then Moses called all the elders of Israel together and told them, "Get the animals for your families and kill the lamb for the Passover. Take a branch of the hyssop plant, dip it into the bowl filled with blood, and then wipe the blood on the sides and tops of the doorframes. No one may leave that house until morning. When the Lord goes through Egypt to kill the Egyptians, he will see the blood on the sides and tops of the doorframes, and he will pass over that house. He will not let the one who brings death come into your houses and kill you.

"You must keep this command as a law for you and your descendants from now on. Do this when you go to the land the Lord has promised to give you. When your children ask you, 'Why are we doing these things?' you will say, 'This is the Passover sacrifice to honour the Lord. When we were in Egypt, the Lord passed over the houses of Israel, and when he killed the Egyptians, he saved our homes.'" Then the people bowed down and worshiped the Lord. They did just as the Lord commanded Moses and Aaron.

John 1:29 (WEB)

The next day, he saw Jesus coming to him, and said, "Behold, the Lamb of God, who takes away the sin of the world!"

🧠 Engaging

Sometimes God asks his people to do the strangest things. Put lamb's blood around the door? How is that going to help?

It reads more like one of those medieval 'cures' for gout: tie a sleeping dormouse round your right thumb and paint its ears with honey three times a day. Hmmmn.

Except that some of these cures turn out to be not so mad after all. One ancient remedy for headaches was to chew on willow bark. These days we call it aspirin.

So was there sense behind God's strange instructions?

This was part of a continuing series of powerful images for God's people. It started with Abraham, when God himself provided the lamb. It continued with the tabernacle, with the temple sacrifices, with the Day of Atonement: one who dies in place of another, removing the curtain between God and God's people.

I wonder what they thought of Moses's strange recipe for salvation then. What do we think of it now?

Talking and Listening

To you, O Lord, I lift my soul.

Make your ways known to me, O Lord,
    and teach me your paths.
Lead me in your truth and teach me
    because you are God, my saviour.
        I wait all day long for you.

Remember, O Lord, your compassionate and merciful deeds.
    They have existed from eternity.
Do not remember the sins of my youth or my rebellious ways.
    Remember me, O Lord, in keeping with your mercy and
        your goodness.

For the sake of your name, O Lord,
    remove my guilt, because it is great.
Look at my misery and suffering,
    and forgive all my sins.

Amen.

(from Psalm 25 GW)

16 Saturday

The Big Story

... and that night the firstborn died, and God's people sheltered beneath the blood of the lamb that was slain, and God brooded over his people and did not permit the destroyer to enter their houses, and God's people left Egypt that very night ...

What do you think it sounded like, that night?

Looking Closer

Exodus 12:23, 30-31 (ERV)

At the time the Lord goes through Egypt to kill the firstborn, he will see the blood on the sides and top of each doorframe. Then he will protect that house and not let the Destroyer come into any of your houses and hurt you.

That night someone died in every house in Egypt. Pharaoh, his officials, and all the people of Egypt began to cry loudly. So that night Pharaoh called for Moses and Aaron and said to them, "Get up and leave my people. You and your people can do as you say. Go and worship the Lord."

Psalm 91:1-6 (NIV)

Whoever dwells in the shelter of the Most High
    will rest in the shadow of the Almighty.
I will say of the Lord, "He is my refuge and my fortress,
    my God, in whom I trust."

Surely he will save you from the fowler's snare
    and from the deadly pestilence.
He will cover you with his feathers,
    and under his wings you will find refuge;
    his faithfulness will be your shield and rampart.

You will not fear the terror of night,
    nor the arrow that flies by day,
nor the pestilence that stalks in the darkness,
    nor the plague that destroys at midday.

Engaging

Sheltering under the wings of the Almighty – what a wonderful place to be.

I love this vision of God hovering over (or 'passing over') his people, protecting them from the destroyer. On that night of terror, God sheltered his people, as an eagle shelters its chick, and there, under his wings, they found refuge.

Nowhere does the Bible promise that being a Christian makes everything fine. Christians get cancer at the same rate as everyone else. Christians fail exams and Christians get made redundant.

But God promises that he is always with us, whether things are going well or badly. Valley of shadow? We will still go through it, but not alone.

Talking and Listening

God of my salvation,

I need not fear the terror of night,
  nor the arrow that flies by day
    nor the pestilence that stalks in the darkness,
      nor the plague that destroys at midday.
For you are my refuge and my fortress,
  my God, in whom I trust.

Amen.

Third Sunday in Lent

The Big Story

... but the people came to the waters of the Red Sea and they could not cross, and they heard the horses and chariots of the Egyptians thundering in the distance; and they cried out against Moses saying, "Were there no graves for us in Egypt?"

Perhaps they thought this was the end of the story.
But it was not.

Why do you think the people of Israel lost faith in God so quickly?

🔍 Looking Closer

Exodus 14:5-7, 10-12 (ERV)

Pharaoh received a report that the Israelites had escaped. When he heard this, he and his officials changed their minds about what they had done. Pharaoh said, "Why did we let the Israelites leave? Why did we let them run away? Now we have lost our slaves!"

So Pharaoh prepared his chariot and took his men with him. He took 600 of his best men and all of his chariots. There was an officer in each chariot.

When the Israelites saw Pharaoh and his army coming toward them, they were very frightened and cried to the Lord for help. They said to Moses, "Why did you bring us out of Egypt? Did you bring us out here in the desert to die? We could have died peacefully in Egypt; there were plenty of graves in Egypt. We told you this would happen! In Egypt we said, 'Please don't bother us. Let us stay and serve the Egyptians.' It would have been better for us to stay and be slaves than to come out here and die in the desert."

Psalm 22:1-2, 11-14 (NIV)

For the director of music. To the tune of 'The Doe of the Morning.' A psalm of David.

My God, my God, why have you forsaken me?
 Why are you so far from saving me,
 so far from my cries of anguish?
My God, I cry out by day, but you do not answer,
 by night, but I find no rest.

Do not be far from me,
 for trouble is near
 and there is no one to help.
Many bulls surround me;
 strong bulls of Bashan encircle me.
Roaring lions that tear their prey

open their mouths wide against me.
I am poured out like water,
    and all my bones are out of joint.
My heart has turned to wax;
    it has melted within me.

Engaging

They couldn't see, the people of Israel, they couldn't see anything. They could not see a way forward, nor a way back. No escape, no hope, and no God. They could not see at all.

Funny thing was, there was plenty of light to see by. God had brought them out of Egypt. They were heading for freedom and had come to the Red Sea. How did they get here? By following God - pillar of cloud by day and pillar of fire by night.

Great! You'd think that after such huge miracles they might have understood that God was looking after them. But no.

God even moved the fire-cloud between the Israelites and the pursuing Egyptians and made the cloud light up the night. But the Israelites couldn't see it.

Sure, they could see it with their eyes, but it didn't travel down the optic nerve to their brains. It's like their heads were still in darkness even while their bodies were in the light.

Talking and Listening

Lord God,

Thank you that we can bring our troubles to you.
Thank you that you listen to our sorrows and laments.

Help us to remember that you are greater than our afflictions,
and help us to trust you,
through the big worries as well as the small.

Amen.

Week Four

Paradise Found

Monday

And God sent a strong wind to push back the waters of the Red Sea, and the people of God crossed from slavery to freedom on dry ground, and they travelled through the wilderness and God provided bread of heaven and springs of living water ...

Tuesday

And God led the people to the mountain of God, and gave them ten best rules for life, and God said, "I am to be your top priority, nothing else; respect my name and spend time with me; respect your parents and life and marriage and property and truth, and do not let possessions possess you" ...

Wednesday

And Moses died and Joshua led God's people across the Jordan into the land of promise, and said, "Choose today whom you will worship – the gods of the nations around you or The Lord your God – as for me, I will worship The Lord"; and the people turned away to other gods ...

Thursday

And God's people were oppressed by the nations around and cried out in their misery, and God had pity and raised up judges to rescue them, yet the people soon forgot The Lord and turned to other gods; and Ruth travelled to Bethlehem and said, "your people will be my people and your God, my God", and she became the great-grandmother of David ...

Friday

And Samuel heard God calling in the night and answered, "Speak Lord, your servant is listening", and the people would not hear God and demanded a king like the nations around them; and Samuel anointed Saul, a tall and handsome man, and Saul became powerful and departed from God's ways, and God rejected Saul as king ...

Saturday

And God chose David, a shepherd boy, to be king saying, "mortals look at the outside appearance, but I look at the heart"; and David slew Goliath and led Saul's army, and Saul became angry at David's success and David fled from his wrath; and Saul died and David became king and sang, "The Lord is my shepherd, I need nothing more" ...

Sunday

But David strayed from God's ten best rules for life, and he did wrong, and he covered the wrong with more wrong, and the wrongs grew to a mighty tower that fell and crushed him; and David, the man after God's own heart, knew he had failed the God he loved.

Perhaps he thought this was the end of the story.

But it was not.

17 Monday

The Big Story

... and God sent a strong wind to push back the waters of the Red Sea, and the people of God crossed from slavery to freedom on dry ground, and they travelled through the wilderness and God provided bread of heaven and springs of living water ...

What do you think it looked like, crossing the Red Sea?

🔍 Looking Closer

Exodus 16:2-4 (NIV)

In the desert the whole community grumbled against Moses and Aaron. The Israelites said to them, "If only we had died by the Lord's hand in Egypt! There we sat round pots of meat and ate all the food we wanted, but you have brought us out into this desert to starve this entire assembly to death."

Then the Lord said to Moses, "I will rain down bread from heaven for you. The people are to go out each day and gather enough for that day. In this way I will test them and see whether they will follow my instructions."

John 6:5-11, 32-35 (GW)

As Jesus saw a large crowd coming to him, he said to Philip, "Where can we buy bread for these people to eat?" Jesus asked this question to test him. He already knew what he was going to do. Philip answered, "We would need about a year's wages to buy enough bread for each of them to have a piece."

One of Jesus' disciples, Andrew, who was Simon Peter's brother, told him, "A boy who has five loaves of barley bread and two small fish is here. But they won't go very far for so many people." Jesus said, "Have the people sit down."

The people had plenty of grass to sit on. (There were about 5,000 men in the crowd.) Jesus took the loaves, gave thanks, and distributed them to the people who were sitting there. He did the same thing with the fish. All the people ate as much as they wanted.

Jesus said to them, "I can guarantee this truth: Moses didn't give you bread from heaven, but my Father gives you the true bread from heaven. God's bread is the man who comes from heaven and gives life to the world."

They said to him, "Sir, give us this bread all the time."

Jesus told them, "I am the bread of life. Whoever comes to me will never become hungry, and whoever believes in me will never become thirsty."

Engaging

Whinge, whinge, whinge! What a bunch of moaners!

"If only we had died by the Lord's hand in Egypt", they said. Ungrateful much?

"There we sat round pots of meat", they said. (These are the original 'fleshpots'.) Really? Have you forgotten the incidental matter of slavery?

"You have brought us out into this desert to starve", they said. Ummmn, so the huge flocks and herds that you brought with you out of Egypt, are they invisible or something?

Their complaints are completely unreasonable and have no basis in fact. God would be perfectly entitled to tell his people to get a grip and quit bugging him.

But, like a patient parent with a sobbing toddler who is distraught because you cut his cheese into triangles when he wanted squares, God sighs and cuts more cheese. This time in squares.

Talking and Listening

Mighty Loving God,

You give us each day our daily bread,
    and yet we do not live by bread alone.

Thank you that you know our needs
    and provide everything we need to live.

Thank you that you also give us your word,
    so that we may live eternally.

Amen.

18 Tuesday

The Big Story

... and God led the people to the mountain of God, and gave them ten best rules for life, and God said, "I am to be your top priority, nothing else; respect my name and spend time with me; respect your parents and life and marriage and property and truth, and do not let possessions possess you" ...

What rules would you have made?

🔍 Looking Closer

Deuteronomy 5:6-8, 11-12, 16-21 (GW)

"I am the Lord your God, who brought you out of slavery in Egypt.

"Never have any other gods. Never make your own carved idols or statues that represent any creature in the sky, on the earth, or in the water.

"Never use the name of the Lord your God carelessly. The Lord will make sure that anyone who uses his name carelessly will be punished.

"Observe the day of rest as a holy day. This is what the Lord your God has commanded you.

"Honour your father and your mother as the Lord your God has commanded you. Then you will live for a long time, and things will go well for you in the land the Lord your God is giving you.

"Never murder. Never commit adultery. Never steal. Never avoid the truth when you testify about your neighbour. Never desire to take your neighbour's wife away from him. Never long for your neighbour's household, his field, his male or female slave, his ox, his donkey, or anything else that belongs to him."

Mark 12:28-31 (NRSV)

One of the scribes came near and heard them disputing with one another, and seeing that he answered them well, he asked him, "Which commandment is the first of all?" Jesus answered, "The first is, 'Hear, O Israel: the Lord our God, the Lord is one; you shall love the Lord your God with all your heart, and with all your soul, and with all your mind, and with all your strength.' The second is this, 'You shall love your neighbour as yourself.' There is no other commandment greater than these."

Engaging

Even people who have never picked up a Bible in their lives probably know the Ten Commandments. Along with Psalm 23 and The Lord's Prayer, this is one of the famous bits.

It's also one of the most reviled. *"Thou shalt not …"* is how a lot of folks see Christianity – old fashioned, out of date and spoiling my fun.

But let's think about other rules. Fancy a nice game of cards? Pretty tricky if there are no rules. Even worse if some people are playing by one set of rules and some by another. The rules make it fair. Without the rules there is no game.

And the only reason for saying *don't do such-and-such* is that we have a tendency to do it. There is no need for God to say, *"Don't eat soup with chopsticks."* Why would we want to?

So if we squirm under the best rules for life, we only have ourselves to blame.

Talking and Listening

Loving Lord,

You know us better than we know ourselves.
You know that we need good rules for life,
   and you lovingly give us what we need,
But may we follow the spirit of your law,
   and not the letter only,
Loving you with all our heart, soul, mind and strength,
   and others as ourselves.

Amen.

19 Wednesday

The Big Story

… and Joshua led God's people across the Jordan into the land of promise, and said, "Choose today whom you will worship – the gods of the nations around you or The Lord your God – as for me, I will worship The Lord"; and the people turned away to other gods …

Why do you think the people of Israel chose to turn away?

Looking Closer

Joshua 24:14-17 (NCV)

Then Joshua said to the people, "Now respect the Lord and serve him fully and sincerely. Throw away the gods that your ancestors worshiped on the other side of the Euphrates River and in Egypt. Serve the Lord. But if you don't want to serve the Lord, you must choose for yourselves today whom you will serve. You may serve the gods that your ancestors worshiped when they lived on the other side of the Euphrates River, or you may serve the gods of the Amorites who lived in this land. As for me and my family, we will serve the Lord."

Then the people answered, "We will never stop following the Lord to serve other gods! It was the Lord our God who brought our ancestors out of Egypt. We were slaves in that land, but the Lord did great things for us there. He brought us out and protected us while we travelled through other lands."

Matthew 6:6-13, 19-21, 24 (WEB)

But you, when you pray, enter into your inner room, and having shut your door, pray to your Father who is in secret; and your Father who sees in secret will reward you openly. In praying, don't use vain repetitions as the Gentiles do; for they think that they will be heard for their much speaking. Therefore don't be like them, for your Father knows what things you need before you ask him. Pray like this:

"Our Father in heaven, may your name be kept holy.
Let your Kingdom come.
    Let your will be done on earth as it is in heaven.
Give us today our daily bread.
Forgive us our debts,
    as we also forgive our debtors.
Bring us not into temptation,
    but deliver us from the evil one.
For yours is the Kingdom, the power, and the glory forever.
Amen."

"Don't lay up treasures for yourselves on the earth, where moth and rust consume, and where thieves break through and steal; but lay up for yourselves treasures in heaven, where neither moth nor rust consume, and where thieves don't break through and steal; for where your treasure is, there your heart will be also.

"No one can serve two masters, for either he will hate the one and love the other, or else he will be devoted to one and despise the other. You can't serve both God and Mammon."

Engaging

"Choose for yourselves today whom you will serve", said Joshua as God's people got ready to settle in their new land. It had to be their choice. You can't *make* someone love God.

Sure, they could go through the motions, but were their hearts in it? (A recurring theme for many later prophets.) This was an opportunity for a fresh start. Walking the walk instead of just talking the talk.

Jesus said the same thing, *"Where your treasure is, there your heart will be also"*. Treasure boxes might contain money, or elusive youth, prestige, finding 'the one' or something else.

Choose for yourselves today.

Talking and Listening

Our Father in heaven, may your name be kept holy.
Let your Kingdom come.
    Let your will be done on earth as it is in heaven.
Give us today our daily bread.
Forgive us our debts,
    as we also forgive our debtors.
Bring us not into temptation,
    but deliver us from the evil one.
For yours is the Kingdom, the power, and the glory forever.
Amen.

20 Thursday

The Big Story

... and God's people were oppressed by the nations around and cried out in their misery, and God had pity and raised up judges to rescue them, yet the people soon forgot The Lord and turned to other gods; and Ruth travelled to Bethlehem and said, "your people will be my people and your God, my God", and she became the great-grandmother of David ...

Why do you think Ruth chose to follow the God of Israel?

🔍 Looking Closer

Judges 2:7, 10-11, 16-19 (NRSV)

The people worshiped the Lord all the days of Joshua, and all the days of the elders who outlived Joshua, who had seen all the great work that the Lord had done for Israel.

Moreover, that whole generation was gathered to their ancestors, and another generation grew up after them, who did not know the Lord or the work that he had done for Israel. Then the Israelites did what was evil in the sight of the Lord and worshiped the Baals;

Then the Lord raised up judges, who delivered them out of the power of those who plundered them. Yet they did not listen even to their judges; for they lusted after other gods and bowed down to them. They soon turned aside from the way in which their ancestors had walked, who had obeyed the commandments of the Lord; they did not follow their example.

Whenever the Lord raised up judges for them, the Lord was with the judge, and he delivered them from the hand of their enemies all the days of the judge; for the Lord would be moved to pity by their groaning because of those who persecuted and oppressed them. But whenever the judge died, they would relapse and behave worse than their ancestors, following other gods, worshiping them and bowing down to them. They would not drop any of their practices or their stubborn ways.

Ruth 1:1, 3-5, 15-16 (GW)

In the days when the judges were ruling, there was a famine in the land. A man from Bethlehem in Judah went with his wife and two sons to live for a while in the country of Moab.

Now, Naomi's husband Elimelech died, and she was left alone with her two sons. Each son married a woman from Moab. One son married a woman named Orpah, and the other son married a woman named Ruth. They lived there for about ten years. Then both Mahlon and Chilion died as well. So Naomi was left alone, without her two sons or her husband.

Naomi said, "Look, your sister-in-law has gone back to her people and to her gods. Go back with your sister-in-law."

But Ruth answered, "Don't force me to leave you. Don't make me turn back from following you. Wherever you go, I will go, and wherever you stay, I will stay. Your people will be my people, and your God will be my God."

Engaging

God's people are a bit of a mixed bunch. We come in every size, shape and colour (whether that refers to skin, political party or football team). There are flavours of Christianity so different that you'd be hard pressed to spot similarities beyond *"We believe in one God ..."*

But what about in the past? God's people were just one race, back in the Old Testament. Weren't they?

Bluntly, no. Ruth was a Moabite, definitely not one of God's people, yet here she is, joining the family. And I mean THE family. Ruth is the reason that we sing 'O Little Town of Bethlehem' at Christmas, and she's not the only foreigner in Jesus' family tree.

Even the people who left Egypt with Moses was a 'mixed multitude' of Israelites and others. God does not seem to mind all kinds of people joining him – not now, not ever.

Talking and Listening

Lord of all the Earth,

Thank you that your family is large enough for all.
Help us to remember that your son Jesus welcomed the outcast and ate with those rejected by society.
May we offer gracious acceptance to all,
just as you have in Christ, accepted us.

Amen.

21 Friday

The Big Story

... and Samuel heard God calling in the night and answered, "Speak Lord, your servant is listening", and the people would not hear God and demanded a king like the nations around them; and Samuel anointed Saul, a tall and handsome man, and Saul became powerful and departed from God's ways, and God rejected Saul as king ...

What do you think is was like for Samuel, hearing God's voice in the night?

Looking Closer

1 Samuel 3:1, 3-10 (GW)

The boy Samuel was serving the Lord under Eli. In those days a prophecy from the Lord was rare; visions were infrequent. The lamp in God's temple hadn't gone out yet, and Samuel was asleep in the temple of the Lord where the ark of God was kept. Then the Lord called Samuel.

"Here I am", Samuel responded. He ran to Eli and said, "Here I am. You called me." "I didn't call you", Eli replied. "Go back to bed." So Samuel went back and lay down.

The Lord called Samuel again. Samuel got up, went to Eli, and said, "Here I am. You called me." "I didn't call you, son", he responded. "Go back to bed." Samuel had no experience with the Lord, because the Lord's word had not yet been revealed to him.

The Lord called Samuel a third time. Samuel got up, went to Eli, and said, "Here I am. You called me." Then Eli realized that the Lord was calling the boy. "Go, lie down", Eli told Samuel. "When he calls you, say, 'Speak, Lord. I'm listening.'" So Samuel went and lay down in his room.

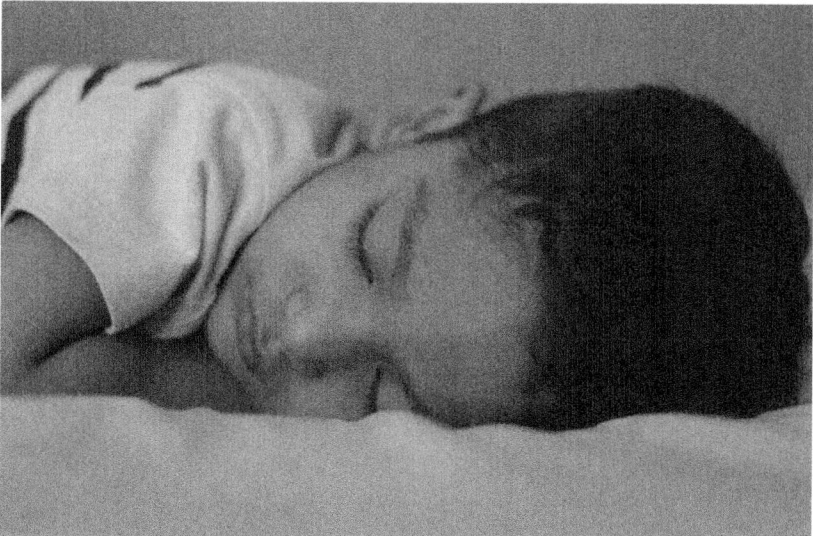

The Lord came and stood there. He called as he had called the other times: "Samuel! Samuel!" And Samuel replied, "Speak. I'm listening."

Psalm 62:5-7 (NRSV)

For God alone my soul waits in silence,
    for my hope is from him.
He alone is my rock and my salvation,
my fortress; I shall not be shaken.
On God rests my deliverance and my honour;
    my mighty rock, my refuge is in God.

Engaging

Waiting in silence. I'm pretty rubbish at that.

I try, really I do, but my mind is full of the jumble of the day – I must remember to put the washing on, the car tax is due soon, my knee is aching again, I hope it's not something serious, where's that form I need to fill in?

I imagine it was much the same for Eli. Different time, same jumble – I must remember to put the shewbread out, the incense needs changing soon, my knee is aching again, I hope it's not something serious, where's that scroll I need to fill in?

But Samuel seems to have the knack of hearing God above the jumble. I wonder how he did it.

Talking and Listening

Gentle Spirit of God,

Still my heart that I may know you,
    Focus my eyes that I may see you.
        Calm my mind that I may hear your guiding voice
            and when I hear,
                may I follow.

Amen.

22 Saturday

The Big Story

... and God chose David, a shepherd boy, to be king saying, "mortals look at the outside appearance, but I look at the heart"; and David slew Goliath and led Saul's army, and Saul became angry at David's success and David fled from his wrath; and Saul died and David became king and sang, "The Lord is my shepherd, I need nothing more" ...

What song would you sing?

Looking Closer

1 Samuel 16:1, 6-12 (MSG)

God addressed Samuel: "So, how long are you going to mope over Saul? You know I've rejected him as king over Israel. Fill your flask with anointing oil and get going. I'm sending you to Jesse of Bethlehem. I've spotted the very king I want among his sons."

When they arrived, Samuel took one look at Eliab and thought, "Here he is! God's anointed!" But God told Samuel, "Looks aren't everything. Don't be impressed with his looks and stature. I've already eliminated him. God judges persons differently than humans do. Men and women look at the face; God looks into the heart."

Jesse then called up Abinadab and presented him to Samuel. Samuel said, "This man isn't God's choice either." Next Jesse presented Shammah. Samuel said, "No, this man isn't either."

Jesse presented his seven sons to Samuel. Samuel was blunt with Jesse, "God hasn't chosen any of these." Then he asked Jesse, "Is this it? Are there no more sons?" "Well, yes, there's the runt. But he's out tending the sheep."

Samuel ordered Jesse, "Go get him. We're not moving from this spot until he's here." Jesse sent for him. He was brought in, the very picture of health—bright-eyed, good-looking.

God said, "Up on your feet! Anoint him! This is the one."

Psalm 23 (NCV)

A psalm of David.
The Lord is my shepherd;
    I have everything I need.
He lets me rest in green pastures.
    He leads me to calm water.
He gives me new strength.
He leads me on paths that are right
    for the good of his name.

Even if I walk through a very dark valley,
  I will not be afraid,
because you are with me.
  Your rod and your shepherd's staff comfort me.

You prepare a meal for me
  in front of my enemies.
You pour oil of blessing on my head;
  you fill my cup to overflowing.
Surely your goodness and love will be with me all my life,
and I will live in the house of the Lord forever.

Engaging

Israel had asked for a king, and God had given them one, but it hadn't turned out very well. Saul had drifted away from God and ruled in his own wisdom. So we 'turn it off, then turn it back on', reboot and try again. God tells Samuel to anoint a new king, and it turns out to be young David.

It must have been a bit of a shock for the lad. For starters, Saul was still king, and David was just a teenager, minding the sheep for his dad. Bit of a Cinderella, really. They didn't even bother to call him in for the ceremonial shoe-fitting. Then Zap! "You shall go to the ball!" says Samuel.

Not at all what David would have imagined as he sat with the sheep, writing, "The Lord is my shepherd ..."

Talking and Listening

Loving Lord,

May I learn to see you in the ordinary things of my life.
May I hear your voice as I go about my tasks.
May I sense your glory in my everyday surroundings
May I know your presence as I rise and as I sit,
  as I go out and come in, as I wake and as I sleep.

Amen.

Fourth Sunday in Lent

The Big Story

... but David strayed from God's ten best rules for life, and he did wrong, and he covered the wrong with more wrong, and the wrongs grew to a mighty tower that fell and crushed him; and David, the man after God's own heart, knew he had failed the God he loved.

Perhaps he thought this was the end of the story.
But it was not.

How do you cope when you fail God?

🔍 Looking Closer

2 Samuel 12:1-9, 13a (GW)

So the Lord sent Nathan to David. Nathan came to him and said, "There were two men in a certain city. One was rich, and the other was poor. The rich man had a very large number of sheep and cows, but the poor man had only one little female lamb that he had bought. He raised her, and she grew up in his home with his children. She would eat his food and drink from his cup. She rested in his arms and was like a daughter.

"Now, a visitor came to the rich man. The rich man thought it would be a pity to take one of his own sheep or cattle to prepare a meal for the traveller. So he took the poor man's lamb and prepared her for the traveller."

David burned with anger against the man. "I solemnly swear, as the Lord lives", he said to Nathan, "the man who did this certainly deserves to die! And he must pay back four times the price of the lamb because he did this and had no pity."

"You are the man!" Nathan told David. "This is what the Lord God of Israel says: I anointed you king over Israel and rescued you from Saul. I gave you your master Saul's house and his wives. I gave you the house of Israel and Judah. And if this weren't enough, I would have given you even more. Why did you despise my word by doing what I considered evil? You had Uriah the Hittite killed in battle. You took his wife as your wife. You used the Ammonites to kill him."

Then David said to Nathan, "I have sinned against the Lord."

1 John 1:8-10 (WEB)

If we say that we have no sin, we deceive ourselves, and the truth is not in us. If we confess our sins, he is faithful and righteous to forgive us the sins, and to cleanse us from all unrighteousness. If we say that we haven't sinned, we make him a liar, and his word is not in us.

Engaging

I can remember a feeling of morbid dread as a child. I had done something wrong and was terrified of being found out.

OK, I hadn't murdered someone to marry his wife, I'd stayed in the school library after lunchtime, but I was in utter terror of every passing footstep. I hid in a crevice behind the bookshelves, lying in the dust and dark for hours until I heard the bell for end of school.

I wonder what was going through David's mind in the days and weeks before Nathan's devastating denouncement, "*You are that man!*" Surely David already knew? Surely this 'man after God's own heart' realised what he was doing?

But somehow, he managed to ignore his conscience, silence the warning bells and ignore the flashing red lights. It's worrying, because if someone that close to God can lie to themselves so successfully, it makes me wonder what blind spots I have in my own life. Where am I deceiving myself? Am I still reading in the library, blithely ignoring the bell that says, "It's time to stop"?

Talking and Listening

Loving Father,

I know that there is much about me that needs fixing,
but I thank you that you do not fix it all at once,
for that would be overwhelming.
Please help me to hear the voice inside
prompting me to change something
that yesterday was acceptable.
I when I hear, to obey.

Amen.

Week Five

Paradise Lost

Monday

And David confessed his wrong and turned back to God, and God created a clean heart in David and took his sin further away than the east is from the west, for The Lord is compassionate and gracious, slow to anger and overflowing with strong and steady love ...

Tuesday

And David's son, Solomon, became king, and Solomon built a temple for The Lord his God; and became rich and wandered from God's ways and followed the gods of the nations around; and God divided Solomon's kingdom in two: Israel and Judah; and many kings came after who did not follow The Lord their God ...

Wednesday

And God called Elijah to turn the hearts of the people back to The Lord their God, and Elijah mocked the prophets of Baal whose sacrifice lay untouched saying, "Perhaps your god is on holiday!", and Elijah's offering was consumed by fire from heaven ...

Thursday

And Elijah fled from the king's anger, exhausted and afraid, and an angel tended him; and Elijah came to the mountain of God, and God spoke to Elijah – not in the wind that shattered rocks, nor in the earthquake, nor in the fire, but in the sound of utter silence ...

Friday

And God called Isaiah saying, "Whom shall I send, and who will go for us?" and Isaiah replied, "Here am I, send me"; and God sent Isaiah to draw the peoples' hearts back to The Lord their God; and Isaiah warned of exile and spoke of God's rescue and of a child named 'God is with us', 'Wonderful Counsellor', 'Prince of Peace' ...

Saturday

And still the kingdom of Israel still turned away from God: they trusted in human strength, they chased after false idols and themselves became false, and God sent Assyrian armies and removed them from his sight, and they were gone; and the armies also threatened the kingdom of Judah, and the king called upon The Lord, and The Lord rescued them ...

Sunday

But despite the words of the prophets, and the kings who followed God's ways, eventually Judah also turned away from The Lord their God; and God sent them into captivity in a foreign land, and God's temple was destroyed, and for seventy years the people of God mourned for Jerusalem beside the river in Babylon ...

Perhaps they thought this was the end of the story.

But it was not.

23 Monday

The Big Story

... and David confessed his wrong and turned back to God, and God created a clean heart in David and took his sin further away than the east is from the west, for The Lord is compassionate and gracious, slow to anger and overflowing with strong and steady love ...

Why do you think God is like this?

🔍 Looking Closer

Psalm 51 (GW)

For the choir director; a psalm by David when the prophet Nathan came to him after David's adultery with Bathsheba.

Have pity on me, O God, in keeping with your mercy.
    In keeping with your unlimited compassion, wipe out my rebellious acts.

Wash me thoroughly from my guilt,
        and cleanse me from my sin.
            I admit that I am rebellious.
            My sin is always in front of me.
I have sinned against you, especially you.
I have done what you consider evil.
        So you hand down justice when you speak,
            and you are blameless when you judge.

Indeed, I was born guilty.
        I was a sinner when my mother conceived me.
Yet, you desire truth and sincerity.
        Deep down inside me you teach me wisdom.
Purify me from sin with hyssop, and I will be clean.
Wash me, and I will be whiter than snow.
        Let me hear sounds of joy and gladness.
        Let the bones that you have broken dance.
Hide your face from my sins,
        and wipe out all that I have done wrong.

Create a clean heart in me, O God,
        and renew a faithful spirit within me.
Do not force me away from your presence,
        and do not take your Holy Spirit from me.
Restore the joy of your salvation to me,
        and provide me with a spirit of willing obedience.

Then I will teach your ways to those who are rebellious,
        and sinners will return to you.
You are not happy with any sacrifice.

Otherwise, I would offer one to you.
You are not pleased with burnt offerings.
    The sacrifice pleasing to God is a broken spirit.
    O God, you do not despise a broken and sorrowful heart.

Romans 3:21-26 (ERV)

But God has a way to make people right, and it has nothing to do with the law. He has now shown us that new way, which the law and the prophets told us about. God makes people right through their faith in Jesus Christ.

He does this for all who believe in Christ. Everyone is the same. All have sinned and are not good enough to share God's divine greatness. They are made right with God by his grace. This is a free gift. They are made right with God by being made free from sin through Jesus Christ.

God gave Jesus as a way to forgive people's sins through their faith in him. God can forgive them because the blood sacrifice of Jesus pays for their sins. God gave Jesus to show that he always does what is right and fair. He was right in the past when he was patient and did not punish people for their sins. And in our own time he still does what is right. God worked all this out in a way that allows him to judge people fairly and still make right any person who has faith in Jesus.

Engaging

Kintsugi is the Japanese art of mending broken pots with gold.

Rather than throwing away a dropped plate or bowl, the gaps are filled with gold lacquer and the joins are not hidden, but honoured. The vessel is considered more worthy for having come through the experience.

Apart from being stunningly beautiful to look at, I think the concept of Kintsugi is very healthy.

We're all of us broken pots, but God does not throw us on the scrap heap when we're damaged, whether we're a little bit chipped, moderately cracked or smashed to tiny fragments.

Instead, God lovingly rebuilds us, restores and beautifies us, making us into something that we could not otherwise have become.

💬 Talking and Listening

Gentle Saviour,

We acknowledge your right and authority to judge.
  We recognise the justice and righteousness of your law.
    We submit to your true and faultless verdict.

We are awed by your mercy as you gather our broken lives.
  We are dazzled by your grace as you restore us once again.
    We are astounded by your compassion as you imbue us
      with your own self and make us new.

May we strive to live up to your calling.

Amen.

24 Tuesday

The Big Story

… and David's son, Solomon, became king, and Solomon built a temple for The Lord his God; and became rich and wandered from God's ways and followed the gods of the nations around; and God divided Solomon's kingdom in two: Israel and Judah; and many kings came after who did not follow The Lord their God …

Why do you think Solomon built a temple then left God's ways?

Looking Closer

1 Kings 11:1-6, 11-13 (NRSV)

King Solomon loved many foreign women along with the daughter of Pharaoh: Moabite, Ammonite, Edomite, Sidonian, and Hittite women, from the nations concerning which the Lord had said to the Israelites, "You shall not enter into marriage with them, neither shall they with you; for they will surely incline your heart to follow their gods"; Solomon clung to these in love.

Among his wives were seven hundred princesses and three hundred concubines; and his wives turned away his heart. For when Solomon was old, his wives turned away his heart after other gods; and his heart was not true to the Lord his God, as was the heart of his father David. For Solomon followed Astarte the goddess of the Sidonians, and Milcom the abomination of the Ammonites.

So Solomon did what was evil in the sight of the Lord, and did not completely follow the Lord, as his father David had done.

Mark 10:17-27 (GW)

As Jesus was coming out to the road, a man came running to him and knelt in front of him. He asked Jesus, "Good Teacher, what should I do to inherit eternal life?"

Jesus said to him, "Why do you call me good? No one is good except God alone. You know the commandments: Never murder. Never commit adultery. Never steal. Never give false testimony. Never cheat. Honour your father and mother."

The man replied, "Teacher, I've obeyed all these commandments since I was a boy." Jesus looked at him and loved him. He told him, "You're still missing one thing. Sell everything you have. Give the money to the poor, and you will have treasure in heaven. Then follow me!"

When the man heard that, he looked unhappy and went away sad, because he owned a lot of property. Jesus looked around and said to his disciples, "How hard it will be for rich people to enter God's kingdom!"

The disciples were stunned by his words. But Jesus said to them again, "Children, how hard it is to enter God's kingdom! It is easier for a camel to go through the eye of a needle than for a rich person to enter God's kingdom."

This amazed his disciples more than ever. They asked each other, "Who, then, can be saved?" Jesus looked at them and said, "It's impossible for people to save themselves, but it's not impossible for God to save them. Everything is possible for God."

Engaging

We move from David to his famous son, Solomon. His name is a by-word for wise judgement, but not always, it seems.

At the start of his reign, Solomon asked God for wisdom rather than worldly power, fame or riches. God gave him wisdom, and threw in the others for good measure. But these blessings became a snare to Solomon, and he lost his focus on God.

Solomon built a beautiful temple, and the account of its dedication includes the amusing detail that the priests had to halt the service because God turned up in all his glory!

Nevertheless, God does not live in temples made by human hands, but in hearts. And Solomon's heart had become filled with other things. For where your treasure is ...

Talking and Listening

Lord Jesus,

May our treasure and our hearts always be with you.

Amen.

25 Wednesday

The Big Story

… and God called Elijah to turn the hearts of the people back to The Lord their God, and Elijah mocked the prophets of Baal whose sacrifice lay untouched saying, "Perhaps your god is on holiday!", and Elijah's offering was consumed by fire from heaven …

What would it have been like, do you think?

Looking Closer

1 Kings 18:21, 25-27, 29-30, 33-38 (NIV)

Elijah went before the people and said, "How long will you waver between two opinions? If the Lord is God, follow him; but if Baal is God, follow him."

But the people said nothing.

Elijah said to the prophets of Baal, "Choose one of the bulls and prepare it first, since there are so many of you. Call on the name of your god, but do not light the fire." So they took the bull given them and prepared it.

Then they called on the name of Baal from morning till noon. "Baal, answer us!" they shouted. But there was no response; no one answered. And they danced around the altar they had made. At noon Elijah began to taunt them. "Shout louder!" he said. "Surely he is a god! Perhaps he is deep in thought, or busy, or traveling. Maybe he is sleeping and must be awakened."

Midday passed, and they continued their frantic prophesying until the time for the evening sacrifice. But there was no response, no one answered, no one paid attention.

Then Elijah said to all the people, "Come here to me." They came to him, and he repaired the altar of the Lord, which had been torn down. He arranged the wood, cut the bull into pieces and laid it on the wood. Then he said to them, "Fill four large jars with water and pour it on the offering and on the wood."

"Do it again", he said, and they did it again. "Do it a third time", he ordered, and they did it the third time. The water ran down around the altar and even filled the trench.

At the time of sacrifice, the prophet Elijah stepped forward and prayed: "Lord, the God of Abraham, Isaac and Israel, let it be known today that you are God in Israel and that I am your servant and have done all these things at your command. Answer me, Lord, answer me, so these people will know that you, Lord, are God, and that you are turning their hearts back again."

Then the fire of the Lord fell and burned up the sacrifice, the wood, the stones and the soil, and also licked up the water in the trench.

Acts 26:13-18 (ERV)

On the way there, at noon, I saw a light from heaven, brighter than the sun. It shined all around me and those traveling with me. We all fell to the ground. Then I heard a voice talking to me in Aramaic. The voice said, "Saul, Saul, why are you persecuting me? You are only hurting yourself by fighting me."

I said, "Who are you, Lord?"

The Lord said, "I am Jesus. I am the one you are persecuting. Stand up! I have chosen you to be my servant. You will tell people about me—what you have seen today and what I will show you. This is why I have come to you. I will keep you safe from your own people and from the non-Jewish people, the ones I am sending you to. You will make them able to understand the truth. They will turn away from darkness to the light. They will turn away from the power of Satan, and they will turn to God. Then their sins can be forgiven, and they can be given a place among God's people—those who have been made holy by believing in me."

Engaging

Sometimes, God just kicks bottom! Elijah on Mount Carmel, Paul on the road to Damascus, Moses, Jonah, Jericho, Red Sea ... there are times when God pulls out the fireworks and give us a jaw-dropping display of his might and majesty.

But most of the time, God is more understated. That's very kind of him. I'm not sure I could cope with Elijah-style firebolts from heaven on a daily basis. Although on the plus side, I'd be certain to notice them, and it's a very quick way to get your barbeque lit!

The problem with the understated message is that I'm a bit hard-of-hearing. Or rather, hard-of-noticing.

It's like with Moses. Famously good at hearing God (at least in later life), but I wonder how many times God had tried to get his attention before resorting to the non-flammable bush trick.

Perhaps God had tried before with other odd phenomena, but Moses hadn't noticed, being too busy counting his sheep. Did God attempt to speak to Moses through dreams, only to have Moses pass them off as too much cheese before bed? Had God tried to catch his attention in the quiet moments of the day, but found that Moses was filling that time with listening to the cricket highlights?

I suspect that I miss God's voice when I do similar things (except not the cricket). I may not need a hearing aid just yet, but unless I want the firebolts from heaven, perhaps I need a noticing-aid.

Talking and Listening

Majestic Lord,
    You sit astride the cherubim and ride the wings of the storm.
        May we rightly fear you and reverence your holy name.

Patient Saviour,
    You enter our hearts humbly, as servant to your subjects.
        May we take your yoke and learn from you.

Gentle Spirit,
    You quicken our hearts and lead us into all truth.
        May we be ever filled and re-filled with your power.

Holy God,
    awesome in majesty and perfect in gentleness,
        may we learn to hear your voice
            in the stillness and in the thunder.

Amen.

26 Thursday

The Big Story

and Elijah fled from the king's anger, exhausted and afraid, and an angel tended him; and Elijah came to the mountain of God, and God spoke to Elijah – not in the wind that shattered rocks, nor in the earthquake, nor in the fire, but in the sound of utter silence ...

Why do you think God was in the silence but not the earthquake, wind or fire?

Looking Closer

1 Kings 19:4-6, 9, 11-12 (NRSV)

[Elijah] himself went a day's journey into the wilderness, and came and sat down under a solitary broom tree. He asked that he might die: "It is enough; now, O Lord, take away my life, for I am no better than my ancestors." Then he lay down under the broom tree and fell asleep. Suddenly an angel touched him and said to him, "Get up and eat." He looked, and there at his head was a cake baked on hot stones, and a jar of water. He ate and drank, and lay down again. At that place he came to a cave, and spent the night there.

Then the word of the Lord came to him, saying, "What are you doing here, Elijah? Go out and stand on the mountain before the Lord, for the Lord is about to pass by." Now there was a great wind, so strong that it was splitting mountains and breaking rocks in pieces before the Lord, but the Lord was not in the wind; and after the wind an earthquake, but the Lord was not in the earthquake; and after the earthquake a fire, but the Lord was not in the fire; and after the fire a sound of sheer silence.

Psalm 46:1-2, 10 (WEB)

For the Chief Musician. By the sons of Korah. According to Alamoth.

God is our refuge and strength,
    a very present help in trouble.
Therefore we won't be afraid,
    though the earth changes,
though the mountains are shaken
    into the heart of the seas;

Be still, and know that I am God.
    I will be exalted among the nations.
    I will be exalted in the earth.

Engaging

Elijah is exhausted physically, mentally and spiritually. He is ready to give up on everything. But at the end of his tether, he cries out to God. And God listens.

It's OK to be not OK. Yes, even for Christians. Even for Christian leaders. Even for mighty men and women of God.

Mental hurts are just as valid as physical hurts, and God recognises this in Elijah. He also knows that we are connected creatures. Our bodies affect our minds, and our minds affect our bodies. So God gives Elijah rest and food. And rest and food. And space. And validation.

God listens to Elijah's exhausted lament. He does not retort with a sharp, "Pull yourself together!" but neither does he allow Elijah to wallow in self-pity.

Instead, God gives Elijah a new perspective himself. Elijah knew the Lord Almighty of the violent wind, earthquake and fire, but after the fire came something new. The sound of utter silence, and in the silence, Elijah meets God.

Talking and Listening

Blessed are you, Lord our God,
　　king of the universe,
for your awesome power and majesty
　　are displayed in earthquake, wind and fire,
　　　　yet you know and care for each one of us
　　　　　and speak in a still, small voice.
Grant us grace to find a new experience of you today.
　　In your name we pray.

Amen.

27 Friday

The Big Story

... and God called Isaiah saying, "Whom shall I send, and who will go for us?" and Isaiah replied, "Here am I, send me"; and God sent Isaiah to draw the peoples' hearts back to The Lord their God; and Isaiah warned of exile and spoke of God's rescue and of a child named 'God is with us', 'Wonderful Counsellor', 'Prince of Peace' ...

How would you have answered the call?

🔍 Looking Closer

Isaiah 9:6-7 (NIV)

For to us a child is born,
   to us a son is given,
      and the government will be on his shoulders.
And he will be called
      Wonderful Counsellor, Mighty God,
      Everlasting Father, Prince of Peace.

Of the greatness of his government and peace
      there will be no end.
He will reign on David's throne
      and over his kingdom,
establishing and upholding it
      with justice and righteousness
      from that time on and forever.

The zeal of the Lord Almighty
      will accomplish this.

John14:27 (NCV)

I leave you peace; my peace I give you.

I do not give it to you as the world does. So don't let your hearts
be troubled or afraid.

🧠 Engaging

David's once healthy and hearty kingdom was now a sick and
weak old man. First Solomon had drifted from the Lord's ways,
then his son had drifted further, and finally the kingdom had
split in two. Ten northern tribes rebelled against the king and set
up a rival nation called Israel, while the remaining two southern
tribes took the name of Judah.

Judah's kings turned out to be a mixed bunch, while Israel's
were almost universally dreadful.

Now the tiny country of Judah was being threatened by neighbouring forces, including their brothers in the north.

Peace was in very short supply.

Into this context strides Isaiah who, unlike me, is very long-sighted. This passage is usually read at Christmas, but when Isaiah wrote it, that was still 700 years in the future. Isaiah was speaking into his situation and looking forward to a time of peace for Israel and Judah under one godly king.

The job of a prophet is not divine fortune-teller, but seeing the world through God's eyes and speaking his words into a situation. More forth-telling than fore-telling if you like. But while Isaiah's words were not originally addressed to our situation, they can speak into our lives.

We see Isaiah's vision of a coming righteous king fulfilled in Jesus, our Prince of Peace.

We who once were not God's people, have become God's people, reconciled to God by his blood. And so we have peace with God and with each other.

"For he himself is our peace, who has made the two groups one and has destroyed the barrier, the dividing wall of hostility." (Ephesians 2:14 NIV)

Talking and Listening

Everlasting Father, we worship you.
  Prince of Peace, we worship you.
    Wonderful Counsellor, we worship you.

Mighty God, we worship you;
  three in one, and one in three,
    we worship you Lord, Trinity.

Amen.

28 Saturday

The Big Story

... and still the kingdom of Israel still turned away from God: they trusted in human strength, they chased after false idols and themselves became false, and God sent Assyrian armies and removed them from his sight, and they were gone; and the armies also threatened the kingdom of Judah, and the king called upon The Lord, and The Lord rescued them ...

If you had been God, what would you have done?

🔍 Looking Closer

2 Kings 17:12-15, 22-23 (NIV)

They worshiped idols, though the Lord had said, "You shall not do this." The Lord warned Israel and Judah through all his prophets and seers: "Turn from your evil ways. Observe my commands and decrees, in accordance with the entire Law that I commanded your ancestors to obey and that I delivered to you through my servants the prophets."

But they would not listen and were as stiff-necked as their ancestors, who did not trust in the Lord their God. They rejected his decrees and the covenant he had made with their ancestors and the statutes he had warned them to keep. They followed worthless idols and themselves became worthless. They imitated the nations around them although the Lord had ordered them, "Do not do as they do."

The Israelites persisted in all the sins of Jeroboam and did not turn away from them until the Lord removed them from his presence, as he had warned through all his servants the prophets. So the people of Israel were taken from their homeland into exile in Assyria, and they are still there.

Proverbs 3:5-12 (NCV)

Trust the Lord with all your heart,
   and don't depend on your own understanding.
Remember the Lord in all you do,
   and he will give you success.

Don't depend on your own wisdom.
   Respect the Lord and refuse to do wrong.
Then your body will be healthy,
   and your bones will be strong.

Honour the Lord with your wealth
   and the firstfruits from all your crops.
Then your barns will be full,
   and your wine barrels will overflow with new wine.

My child, do not reject the Lord's discipline,
    and don't get angry when he corrects you.
The Lord corrects those he loves,
    just as parents correct the child they delight in.

Engaging

The kingdom of Israel had a succession of appalling kings. The first, Jeroboam, had rebelled against Solomon's house and established a rival kingdom in the north, with a capital at Samaria. The temple, however, was located in the southern kingdom of Judah, so Jeroboam built two new temples in his northern kingdom, complete with golden calves.

Hmmn, golden calves. Where have I heard that before?

King after rotten king followed, including the notorious Ahab and his wife Jezebel. Each drifted further and further from God's ways, taking the people with them, until they were indistinguishable from the nations around them.

They were the epitome of trusting their own understanding, going through the motions of worshipping the Lord, but it was a god made in their own image. They walked out on God and God, eventually, let them leave.

Talking and Listening

Lord, you have examined me
    and know all about me.
You know when I sit down and when I get up.
    You know my thoughts before I think them.
God, examine me and know my heart;
    test me and know my anxious thoughts.
See if there is any bad thing in me.
    Lead me on the road to everlasting life.

Amen.

(Psalm 139:1-2, 23-24 NCV)

Fifth Sunday in Lent

The Big Story

... but despite the words of the prophets, and the kings who followed God's ways, eventually Judah also turned away from The Lord their God; and God sent them into captivity in a foreign land, and God's temple was destroyed, and for seventy years the people of God mourned for Jerusalem beside the river in Babylon ...

Perhaps they thought this was the end of the story,
But it was not.

How do you think the people felt when the temple was destroyed?

🔍 Looking Closer

2 Chronicles 36:15-20 (GW)

The Lord God of their ancestors repeatedly sent messages through his messengers because he wanted to spare his people and his dwelling place. But they mocked God's messengers, despised his words, and made fun of his prophets until the Lord became angry with his people. He could no longer heal them.

So he had the Babylonian king attack them and execute their best young men in their holy temple. He didn't spare the best men or the unmarried women, the old people or the sick people. God handed all of them over to him. He brought to Babylon each of the utensils from God's temple, the treasures from the Lord's temple, and the treasures of the king and his officials. They burned God's temple, tore down Jerusalem's walls, burned down all its palaces, and destroyed everything of value. The king of Babylon took those who weren't executed to Babylon to be slaves for him and his sons. They remained captives until the Persian Empire began to rule.

Psalm 137:1-4 (NRSV)

By the rivers of Babylon—
    there we sat down and there we wept
    when we remembered Zion.
On the willows there
    we hung up our harps.
For there our captors
    asked us for songs,
and our tormentors asked for mirth, saying,
    "Sing us one of the songs of Zion!"

How could we sing the Lord's song
    in a foreign land?,

Engaging

*"No, No, NO, NO, **NO**! This can't be real! There must be some mistake!"* Disbelief is common when the unthinkable occurs.

I can imagine the people of Jerusalem shouting something similar when they heard that God had finally stopped giving warnings. Now they would see the consequences of their choices. *"Jerusalem destroyed? But ... how can this be?"* The worst thing that could possibly happen, just happened. And it was 100% their own fault.

Hopefully, we won't ever be carried off into exile, but I doubt there are many of us who have not experienced trouble.

Some trouble is of our own making, through poor decisions or deliberate wrong-doing. Some is inflicted on us by others. Other trouble is nobody's fault. Stuff just happens, and sometimes it happens to us.

It's always worth going a bit easy on people. Most of us take pains to hide our scars, so we can never know what wounds other folks are covering.

Talking and Listening

Lord,

Please help me to remember
    that my actions have consequences,
and that while you are gracious and merciful,
    I must not take you for granted.

Please help me to show your grace and mercy
    to those I meet today,
for they are just as much in need of your forgiveness
    as I am.

Amen.

Week Six

The End of Everything

Monday

And the people lived in exile, far from their land; and the prophets spoke of a future hope, of God's sure and gracious plans, of redemption from slavery; and the prophets spoke of a new covenant, of law written on hearts not on stone, of iniquities remembered no more …

Tuesday

And in Babylon the exiles were made to worship the king and gods of that land instead of The Lord their God; and three exiles refused to worship as the world around them, and they were thrown into a furnace of blazing fire; and yet the flames did not touch them and there was one like a son of God who walked with them in the fire …

Wednesday

And generations passed, and God's people waited for the redeemer of whom the prophets spoke, a suffering servant by whose wounds we are healed, one pierced for our transgressions and wounded for our iniquities, a lamb going willingly to sacrifice …

Thursday

And generations passed, and Babylon fell to Persia; and God moved the king of Persia to send the exiles home, and they returned and started to rebuild the temple in Jerusalem; and the prophets spoke of a time when God's spirit would dwell not in temples made of stone, but would live in the hearts of all God's people …

Friday

And there lived in the land some who had not gone into exile, and they had mixed with the nations around and worshipped foreign gods alongside The Lord, and they built a temple in Samaria; and the people of Samaria opposed those who built the temple in Jerusalem, and there was bitter hatred between the Jews and the Samaritans ...

Saturday

And the prophets still spoke of a new Moses, a new David, a new Elijah: born in the city of David, of the house and line of David; who would come as a king on a donkey, as a shepherd to lost sheep, giving sight to the blind and life to the dead; who would beat weapons into farming tools and redeem God's people; Messiah ...

Sunday

But generations passed and the Messiah did not come, and the voices of the prophets were stilled, and the Word of The Lord was heard no more; and God's people wandered in this desert for four hundred years; and all creation waited. In the silence.

Perhaps they thought this was the end of the story.

But it was not.

29 Monday

The Big Story

... and the people lived in exile, far from their land; and the prophets spoke of a future hope, of God's sure and gracious plans, of redemption from slavery; and the prophets spoke of a new covenant, of law written on hearts not on stone, of iniquities remembered no more ...

What does it mean to have law written on your heart?

🔍 Looking Closer

Jeremiah 31:31-34 (NCV)

"Look, the time is coming", says the Lord,
　"when I will make a new agreement
with the people of Israel
　and the people of Judah.
It will not be like the agreement
　I made with their ancestors
when I took them by the hand
　to bring them out of Egypt.
I was a husband to them,
　but they broke that agreement", says the Lord.
"This is the agreement I will make
　with the people of Israel at that time", says the Lord:
"I will put my teachings in their minds
　and write them on their hearts.
I will be their God,
　and they will be my people.
People will no longer have to teach
　their neighbours and relatives
　to know the Lord,
because all people will know me,
　from the least to the most important", says the Lord.
"I will forgive them for the wicked things they did,
　and I will not remember their sins anymore."

Ezekiel 34:11-12, 14-15, 23-24 (GW)

This is what the Almighty Lord says: I will search for my sheep myself, and I will look after them. As a shepherd looks after his flock when he is with his scattered sheep, so I will look after my sheep. I will rescue them on a cloudy and gloomy day from every place where they have been scattered. I will feed them in good pasture, and they will graze on the mountains of Israel. They will rest on the good land where they graze, and they will feed on the best pastures in the mountains of Israel. I will take care of my sheep and lead them to rest, declares the Almighty Lord.

Then I will place one shepherd over them, my servant David, and he will take care of them. He will take care of them and be their shepherd. I, the Lord, will be their God, and my servant David will be their prince. I, the Lord, have spoken.

Engaging

What a dreadful place God's people were in. Not that Babylon was dreadful. It was powerful, prosperous and a seat of great learning and culture. Cambridge, London and the nice bits of New York combined. But they were in a bad place spiritually.

The holy items of God's temple were now Nebuchadnezzar's tableware, so how could they offer sacrifices? The temple itself was destroyed, so how could they worship? They were exiled far from God's land, so how could they pray? Could God even see them, here, in Babylon?

God gives them two beautiful pictures of hope and restoration: God as husband, God as shepherd. "Just as I took you by the hand to lead you out of Egypt", he says, "so I will bring you out from the nations. I will take care of you as a shepherd his sheep, and I will lead you to rest."

Then God speaks of a new way of living. Not by laws written on tablets of stone, but with law written on hearts. And not under a fallible human king, but a godly shepherd-king who would forgive their wickedness and remember their sins no more. "Because all people will know me, from the least to the most important", says the Lord.

Talking and Listening

Blessed are you, Lord our God,
 king of the universe,
  for you are our shepherd-king,
   and we are the sheep of your pasture.
Blessed be your name for ever.

Amen.

30 Tuesday

The Big Story

… and in Babylon the exiles were made to worship the king and gods of that land instead of The Lord their God; and three exiles refused to worship as the world around them, and they were thrown into a furnace of blazing fire; and yet the flames did not touch them and there was one like a son of God who walked with them in the fire …

Who do you think the fourth person in the fire was?

🔍 Looking Closer

Daniel 3:16-20, 24-25

Shadrach, Meshach and Abednego replied to him, "King Nebuchadnezzar, we do not need to defend ourselves before you in this matter. If we are thrown into the blazing furnace, the God we serve is able to deliver us from it, and he will deliver us from Your Majesty's hand. But even if he does not, we want you to know, Your Majesty, that we will not serve your gods or worship the image of gold you have set up."

Then Nebuchadnezzar was furious with Shadrach, Meshach and Abednego, and his attitude toward them changed. He ordered the furnace heated seven times hotter than usual and commanded some of the strongest soldiers in his army to tie up Shadrach, Meshach and Abednego and throw them into the blazing furnace.

Then King Nebuchadnezzar leaped to his feet in amazement and asked his advisers, "Weren't there three men that we tied up and threw into the fire?" They replied, "Certainly, Your Majesty."

He said, "Look! I see four men walking around in the fire, unbound and unharmed, and the fourth looks like a son of the gods."

Romans 8:31-39 (MSG)

So, what do you think? With God on our side like this, how can we lose? If God didn't hesitate to put everything on the line for us, embracing our condition and exposing himself to the worst by sending his own Son, is there anything else he wouldn't gladly and freely do for us? And who would dare tangle with God by messing with one of God's chosen? Who would dare even to point a finger? The One who died for us—who was raised to life for us!—is in the presence of God at this very moment sticking up for us.

Do you think anyone is going to be able to drive a wedge between us and Christ's love for us? There is no way! Not trouble, not hard times, not hatred, not hunger, not homelessness, not bullying threats, not backstabbing, not even the worst sins listed in Scripture:

> They kill us in cold blood because they hate you.
> We're sitting ducks; they pick us off one by one.

None of this fazes us because Jesus loves us. I'm absolutely convinced that nothing—nothing living or dead, angelic or demonic, today or tomorrow, high or low, thinkable or unthinkable—absolutely nothing can get between us and God's love because of the way that Jesus our Master has embraced us.

Engaging

"But even if he does not". What great words. *"But even if he does not"*. Probably the greatest words of grounded faith that I've ever read.

It can sometimes be a tricky balancing act, standing with one foot in this world and one foot in the next. Some of us cope by leaning more on one side than the other. There are the people who are so heavenly minded that they're no earthly use, or the ones Jesus complained about whose treasure was all on earth.

But these three Jewish exiles coped well with the unstable equilibrium. They didn't hop from side to side – good Jewish boys on Sabbath, Babylonian citizens the rest of the week – they lived both lives at the same time. They were realistic about the probable outcome of their actions while still keeping strong in their faith.

Our God is able to rescue us. That is certain.
   Maybe he will, and you'll see God's power.
     Maybe he won't and you'll think you've won,

But you haven't.

Talking and Listening

Faithful God,

Blessed be your name
   in the land that is plentiful,
   where your streams of abundance flow,
Blessed be your name.

Blessed be your name
   when I'm found in the desert place,
   though I walk through the wilderness,
Blessed be your name.

Every blessing you pour out,
   I'll turn back to praise.
When the darkness closes in, Lord
   Still I will say:

Blessed be the name of the Lord,
   Blessed be your name.
Blessed be the name of the Lord,
   Blessed be your glorious name.

Amen.

(Matt Redman)

31 Wednesday

The Big Story

... and generations passed, and God's people waited for the redeemer of whom the prophets spoke, a suffering servant by whose wounds we are healed, one pierced for our transgressions and wounded for our iniquities, a lamb going willingly to sacrifice ...

Does this remind you of anything else from the story of God and God's people?

Looking Closer

Isaiah 53:3-9 (GW)

He was despised and rejected by people.
He was a man of sorrows, familiar with suffering.
He was despised
  like one from whom people turn their faces,
  and we didn't consider him to be worth anything.
He certainly has taken upon himself our suffering
  and carried our sorrows,
    but we thought that God had wounded him,
      beat him, and punished him.
He was wounded for our rebellious acts.
  He was crushed for our sins.
    He was punished so that we could have peace,
      and we received healing from his wounds.

We have all strayed like sheep.
Each one of us has turned to go his own way,
  and the Lord has laid all our sins on him.
He was abused and punished,
  but he didn't open his mouth.
He was led like a lamb to the slaughter.
He was like a sheep that is silent
  when its wool is cut off.
    He didn't open his mouth.

He was arrested, taken away, and judged.
  Who would have thought that he would be removed
from the world?
He was killed because of my people's rebellion.
He was placed in a tomb with the wicked.
He was put there with the rich when he died,
  although he had done nothing violent
    and had never spoken a lie.

Philippians 2:5-11 (ERV)

In your life together, think the way Christ Jesus thought.

He was like God in every way,
  but he did not think that his being equal with God
  was something to use for his own benefit.
Instead, he gave up everything, even his place with God.
  He accepted the role of a servant,
  appearing in human form.
During his life as a man,
  he humbled himself by being fully obedient to God,
  even when that caused his death—death on a cross.
So God raised him up to the most important place
  and gave him the name
  that is greater than any other name.
God did this so that every person
  will bow down to honour the name of Jesus.
  Everyone in heaven, on earth,
  and under the earth will bow.
They will all confess, "Jesus Christ is Lord,"
  and this will bring glory to God the Father.

Engaging

Scapegoat these days has negative connotations of unfair blame, but it was originally a dramatic demonstration of God's mercy.

The word comes from '(e)scape goat', part of the ceremony of the Day of Atonement, where the high priest would lay the sins of God's people on the head of a goat, then send it out into the desert, symbolically carrying their sins away, never to be seen again.

It's a very powerful image.

The goat itself had no choice in the matter, but Jesus offered himself as a willing scapegoat for us all – the lamb of God who takes away the sin of the world.

123

David wrote of this in a psalm:

The Lord is merciful and gracious,
    slow to anger and abounding in steadfast love.
He will not always accuse,
    nor will he keep his anger forever.
He does not deal with us according to our sins,
    nor repay us according to our iniquities.
For as the heavens are high above the earth,
    so great is his steadfast love toward those who fear him;
as far as the east is from the west,
    so far he removes our transgressions from us.

(Psalm 103:8-12 NRSV)

Talking and Listening

Merciful Father,

From time before time you planned it.
    From eternity you made it sure.
        In the life of Jesus you made it known.

Your plan of salvation.
This was no mistake,
    no dreadful accident,
        no plan B.

You showed us from ancient times
    how you would accomplish it.
You gave us time to learn
    to confess,
        to repent,
            to receive forgiveness,
as our sins are taken over the horizon,
    as far as the east is from the west.

Praise be to your name for ever.

Amen.

32 Thursday

The Big Story

… and generations passed, and Babylon fell to Persia; and God moved the king of Persia to send the exiles home, and they returned and started to rebuild the temple in Jerusalem; and the prophets spoke of a time when God's spirit would dwell not in temples made of stone, but would live in the hearts of all God's people …

What does it mean for God's spirit to live in a temple or a heart?

Looking Closer

2 Chronicles 36:20-23 (ERV)

Nebuchadnezzar took the people who were still alive back to Babylon and forced them to be slaves. They stayed in Babylon as slaves until the Persian kingdom defeated the kingdom of Babylon. The land of Judah became an empty desert and stayed that way for 70 years. All this time the land rested to make up for the Sabbath rests that the people had not kept. This is just what the Lord said would happen in the warning he gave through the prophet Jeremiah.

During the first year that Cyrus was king of Persia, the Lord caused Cyrus to make a special announcement. He did this so that what the Lord promised through Jeremiah the prophet would really happen. Cyrus sent messengers to every place in his kingdom. They carried this message:

This is what King Cyrus of Persia says: The Lord, the God of heaven, made me king over the whole earth. He gave me the responsibility of building a Temple for him in Jerusalem. Now, all of you who are his people are free to go to Jerusalem. And may the Lord your God be with you.

Joel 2:25-29 (NIV)

I will repay you for the years the locusts have eaten—
　　the great locust and the young locust,
　　the other locusts and the locust swarm—
my great army that I sent among you.

You will have plenty to eat, until you are full,
　　and you will praise the name of the Lord your God,
　　who has worked wonders for you;
never again will my people be shamed.

Then you will know that I am in Israel,
　　that I am the Lord your God,
　　and that there is no other;
never again will my people be shamed.

And afterward,
   I will pour out my Spirit on all people.
Your sons and daughters will prophesy,
   your old men will dream dreams,
   your young men will see visions.
Even on my servants, both men and women,
   I will pour out my Spirit in those days.

Engaging

In many a movie, the baddies escape the force of the law by crossing the border. Once over the state line, the police have no jurisdiction. People in ancient times often thought that gods worked the same way. They belonged to a place and had no influence outside the borders of that land.

So when the God's people were exiled to Babylon, surely they were out of his reach, beyond his ability to help them? And for certain, no foreign, heathen king could be a tool of God's salvation, could he?

But God reveals, yet again, that he is the God of all people – both Jews and non-Jews, and that *all* kingdoms are his to command.

Talking and Listening

Mighty God,

Praise be to your name for ever and ever;
   wisdom and power are yours.
You change times and seasons;
   you depose kings and raise up others.
You give wisdom to the wise
   and knowledge to the discerning.
Praise be to your name for ever and ever;

Amen.

(From Daniel 2:20-21 NIV)

33 Friday

The Big Story

… and there lived in the land some who had not gone into exile, and they had mixed with the nations around and worshipped foreign gods alongside The Lord, and the people of Samaria opposed the rebuilding, and there was bitter hatred between the Jews and the Samaritans …

Why do you think Jesus chose to tell a story about a good Samaritan?

🔍 Looking Closer

Ezra 4:1-5a (GW)

Many people living in the area [Samaria] were against the people of Judah and Benjamin. These enemies heard that the people who had come from captivity were building a temple for the Lord, the God of Israel. So they came to Zerubbabel and to the family leaders and said, "Let us help you build. We are the same as you, we ask your God for help. We have offered sacrifices to your God since the time King Esarhaddon of Assyria brought us here."

But Zerubbabel, Jeshua, and the other family leaders of Israel answered, "No, you people cannot help us build a temple for our God. Only we can build the Temple for the Lord. He is the God of Israel. This is what King Cyrus of Persia commanded us to do."

So the enemies began to discourage them and tried to frighten them in order to stop them from building the Temple. These enemies hired government officials to work against the people of Judah. The officials constantly did things to stop the Jews' plans to build the Temple.

Luke 10:30-37 (MSG)

Jesus answered by telling a story. "There was once a man traveling from Jerusalem to Jericho. On the way he was attacked by robbers. They took his clothes, beat him up, and went off leaving him half-dead. Luckily, a priest was on his way down the same road, but when he saw him he angled across to the other side. Then a Levite religious man showed up; he also avoided the injured man.

"A Samaritan travelling the road came on him. When he saw the man's condition, his heart went out to him. He gave him first aid, disinfecting and bandaging his wounds. Then he lifted him onto his donkey, led him to an inn, and made him comfortable. In the morning he took out two silver coins and gave them to the innkeeper, saying, 'Take good care of him. If it costs any more, put it on my bill—I'll pay you on my way back.'

"What do you think? Which of the three became a neighbour to the man attacked by robbers?" "The one who treated him kindly", the religion scholar responded.

Jesus said, "Go and do the same."

Engaging

"*Love you neighbour as yourself.*" Sounds simple enough. Nothing too difficult. And nothing new, this comes from right back in Leviticus. Shouldn't be a problem.

"*Yeah, but who is my neighbour?*" Wriggle, wriggle, squirm. "*Surely, Jesus, you don't mean **them**, do you?*"

And Jesus launches into one of the best known of all his stories.

For his first audience, it was shocking. Today, a Samaritan is a helpful person, but back then, they were heretical, sacrilegious pseudo-Jews and you'd cross the road to avoid one.

Samaritans and Jews – they were like Rangers and Celtic, like MacOS and Windows, like Luke Skywalker and Darth Vader.

So if you were a beat-up Jew, the last person you'd want to help you is a filthy Samaritan. "*Urgh! I bet he didn't even wash his hands.*" But it was this outsider who did right in God's eyes.

So, yes, even **them**.

Talking and Listening

Gracious Father

Your love flows wider than my prejudices.
  Your grace reaches beyond people 'like me'.
    Your mercy stretches further than the deserving.
Praise be to your name for ever.

Amen.

34 Saturday

The Big Story

... and the prophets still spoke of a new Moses, a new Elijah, a new David: born in the city of David, of the house and line of David; who would come as a king on a donkey, as a shepherd to lost sheep, giving sight to the blind and life to the dead; who would beat weapons into farming tools and redeem God's people; Messiah ...

What does it mean, a new Moses, a new Elijah, a new David?

🔍 Looking Closer

Malachi 4:1-2a, 5 (MSG)

Count on it: The day is coming, raging like a forest fire. All the arrogant people who do evil things will be burned up like stove wood, burned to a crisp, nothing left but scorched earth and ash— a black day. But for you, sunrise! The sun of righteousness will dawn on those who honour my name, healing radiating from its wings.

But also look ahead: I'm sending Elijah the prophet to clear the way for the Big Day of God—the decisive Judgment Day!

Matthew 16:13-16 (NIV)

When Jesus came to the region of Caesarea Philippi, he asked his disciples, "Who do people say the Son of Man is?" They replied, "Some say John the Baptist; others say Elijah; and still others, Jeremiah or one of the prophets."

"But what about you?" he asked. "Who do you say I am?" Simon Peter answered, "You are the Messiah, the Son of the living God."

Engaging

"Who do you say that I am?"

I've always liked Peter. He can be a bit of a numbskull at times but it's nice to know that even twits can be friends with Jesus.

Peter often demonstrates his chronic foot-in-mouth disease. At the transfiguration, while James and John are awestruck at the splendour of Jesus in glory with Moses and Elijah, Peter blurts out whatever comes first into his head, and that day's daft idea was a glamping site – three little sheds for them each to live in.

Seriously?

But here, Peter's motor-mouth puts into words perhaps what all were thinking but none dared say. *"You are the Messiah, the Son of the living God."*

It's one thing to follow a rabbi, a teacher. It's something quite different to say that your teacher is God's son. Once you've said that, there's no going back.

"Who do you say that I am?"

Talking and Listening

May we have the courage of Peter,
to speak from our hearts
and dare all for you.

Not reserving our judgement,
but voicing the hopes of our hearts

Not standing on our dignity,
but plunging into the water to be near you.

For You are the Messiah, the Son of the living God.

Amen.

Palm Sunday

The Big Story

... but generations passed and the Messiah did not come, and the voices of the prophets were stilled, and the Word of The Lord was heard no more; and God's people wandered in this desert for four hundred years; and all creation waited. In the silence.

Perhaps they thought this was the end of the story.
But it was not.

There are 400 years of silence after the Old Testament and before the New. What do you think was happening between?

🔍 Looking Closer

Zechariah 9:9-10,19 (NCV)

Rejoice greatly, people of Jerusalem!
    Shout for joy, people of Jerusalem!
Your king is coming to you.
    He does what is right, and he saves.
    He is gentle and riding on a donkey,
    on the colt of a donkey.
I will take away the chariots from Ephraim
    and the horses from Jerusalem.
    The bows used in war will be broken.
The king will talk to the nations about peace.
    His kingdom will go from sea to sea,
    and from the Euphrates River to the ends of the earth.

On that day the Lord their God will save them
    as if his people were sheep.
They will shine in his land
    like jewels in a crown.

Matthew 11:2-6, 28-30 (MSG)

John, meanwhile, had been locked up in prison. When he got wind of what Jesus was doing, he sent his own disciples to ask, "Are you the One we've been expecting, or are we still waiting?"

Jesus told them, "Go back and tell John what's going on:

> The blind see,
> The lame walk,
> Lepers are cleansed,
> The deaf hear,
> The dead are raised,
> The wretched of the earth learn that God is on their side.

"Is this what you were expecting? Then count yourselves most blessed!"

135

Engaging

Jesus wasn't the first contender for the title 'messiah', not by a long way, so John's question wasn't unreasonable. Messiah simply means 'anointed one', such as king David and even foreigners like Cyrus, king of Persia, who freed God's people from exile.

In the 400 years between the Old and New Testaments, another popular candidate was Judas Maccabeus. He led a revolt and purified the temple. It was hoped this would throw off the yoke of the occupying forces for good, but by the time of Jesus they were back, this time Roman.

So when Jesus started making waves, many people hoped for a new messiah. A mighty warrior, like Judas Maccabeus, to oust the heathen oppressors and free God's people. Was this him? Was he The One?

Jesus replies with a 'yes' and a 'no'. *"Look at what I'm doing. The blind see. The lame walk. The poor hear the Good News."* Does this sound like the Messiah? Yes. But a mighty warrior king, sword in hand, vanquishing the Romans? Not so much. Not that sort of kingdom.

Talking and Listening

Lord God,

Sometimes we want you to work to our agendas,
    fixing the problems we think want fixing,
        in the way we want them fixed.

But this is your world, not ours.

Please help us to gain your perspective
    one what is important and what is not
        as we live and work in your kingdom.

Amen.

Holy Week

The Beginning of Everything

Monday of Holy Week

And God came as a baby, born to a peasant woman and laid to sleep where animals ate, to rescue the people from their slavery; the eternal Word in frailty of flesh; and John the Baptist's voice was heard in the silence calling, "God's kingdom is come" ...

Tuesday of Holy Week

And Jesus passed through the Jordan as God's people did, and heard God's words; and Jesus was tempted in the wilderness as God's people were, and spoke God's words; and Jesus stood on the mountain shining in the radiance of glory, and God blessed him; and Jesus spoke to the people of the best rules for life saying, "I give you a new commandment" ...

Wednesday of Holy Week

And Jesus said, "I am the Way", and he gave bread to the hungry, water to the thirsty and rest to the weary; and Jesus said, "I am the Light", and he brought sight to the blind, freedom to the prisoner and life to the dead; and Jesus said, "I am the Shepherd", and he welcomed the unwelcome, loved the unlovable and forgave the guilty ...

Maundy Thursday

And Jesus entered Jerusalem as the king of glory proclaiming, "The greatest one is the servant of all"; and he washed the feet of his friends, and broke bread with them saying, "This is the new covenant"; and brought into being the substance of former shadows ...

Good Friday

But Passover came, and the priest became sacrifice to give life to the dead, the master became slave to redeem those in chains, and the perfect Lamb of God gave himself for the wrong of all people; and Jesus spoke forgiveness and welcomed the wanderer home; and darkness covered the land.

They thought this was the end of the story.

But it was not.

Holy Saturday

And and they carried his body to a garden and laid him in a tomb; and there was silence, and in the time between times the world waited, hardly daring even to breathe; and the Ancient of Days gathered the clouds of heaven ...

Easter Sunday

But death could not hold the Lord of Life, and in the darkness of the first day of the week, Jesus burst out and made light and life, and hope and home; and Eden is restored, Jerusalem rebuilt, and the gates of heaven opened; for the old chapter is ended and the new chapter is begun ...

35 Monday of Holy Week

The Big Story

… and God came as a baby, born to a peasant woman and laid to sleep where animals ate, to rescue the people from their slavery; the eternal Word in frailty of flesh; and John the Baptist's voice was heard in the silence calling, "God's kingdom is come" …

What must it have been like, for God to become human?

🔍 Looking Closer

Isaiah 40:1-5 (MSG)

"Comfort, oh comfort my people",
 says your God.
"Speak softly and tenderly to Jerusalem,
 but also make it very clear
That she has served her sentence,
 that her sin is taken care of—forgiven!
She's been punished enough and more than enough,
 and now it's over and done with."

Thunder in the desert!
 "Prepare for God's arrival!
Make the road straight and smooth,
 a highway fit for our God.
Fill in the valleys,
 level off the hills,
Smooth out the ruts,
 clear out the rocks.
Then God's bright glory will shine
 and everyone will see it.
 Yes. Just as God has said."

Galatians 4:4-5 (NRSV)

But when the fullness of time had come, God sent his Son, born of a woman, born under the law, in order to redeem those who were under the law, so that we might receive adoption as children.

🧠 Engaging

It can be easy to look back to some supposed golden age, when everything was right with the world, and to long for a return. At the time of Jesus' birth, many looked back fondly to David's reign, when Israel was a powerful and well-respected nation, ruled by a godly king.

140

So when John the Baptist arrived on the scene, thundering in the desert and saying, "Repent, for the king is coming", it sounded like a return to the glory days.

But this would be a very different type of king.

God was not looking back, but looking forward. This would be no human king, a man after God's own heart, yet still fallible and in need of forgiveness. This would be a king of God's own self, perfect and able to forgive.

Born of woman to be fully like us,
   yet born of God to redeem us.
In our lives and in our world,
   yet bringing our lives and our world into God's kingdom
     heaven to earth and earth to heaven.

Talking and Listening

Father God,

Whom have I in heaven but you?
   And earth has nothing I desire besides you.
My flesh and my heart may fail,
   but God is the strength of my heart
   and my portion forever.
I am always with you;
   you hold me by my right hand.
You guide me with your counsel,
   and afterward you will take me into glory.

Amen.

(Psalm 73:23-26 NIV)

36 Tuesday of Holy Week

The Big Story

… and Jesus passed through the Jordan as God's people did, and heard God's words; and Jesus was tempted in the wilderness as God's people were, and spoke God's words; and Jesus stood on the mountain shining in the radiance of glory, and God blessed him; and Jesus spoke to the people of the best rules for life saying, "I give you a new commandment" …

Why did Jesus get baptised in the Jordan river?

🔍 Looking Closer

Matthew 5:1-10, 17 (WEB)

Seeing the multitudes, he went up onto the mountain. When he had sat down, his disciples came to him. He opened his mouth and taught them, saying,

"Blessed are the poor in spirit,
    for theirs is the Kingdom of Heaven.
Blessed are those who mourn,
    for they shall be comforted.
Blessed are the gentle,
    for they shall inherit the earth.
Blessed are those who hunger and thirst for righteousness,
    for they shall be filled.
Blessed are the merciful,
    for they shall obtain mercy.
Blessed are the pure in heart,
    for they shall see God.
Blessed are the peacemakers,
    for they shall be called children of God.
Blessed are those who have been persecuted for righteousness' sake,
    for theirs is the Kingdom of Heaven.

"Don't think that I came to destroy the law or the prophets. I didn't come to destroy, but to fulfil."

Hebrews 1:1-3 (ERV)

In the past God spoke to our people through the prophets. He spoke to them many times and in many different ways. And now in these last days, God has spoken to us again through his Son. He made the whole world through his Son. And he has chosen his Son to have all things. The Son shows the glory of God. He is a perfect copy of God's nature, and he holds everything together by his powerful command. The Son made people clean from their sins. Then he sat down at the right side of God, the Great One in heaven.

Engaging

When Moses went up the mountain to talk to God, he went alone. The people were afraid to hear God's voice. "*Speak to us yourself*", they said to Moses, "*and we will listen. But don't let God speak to us, or we will die.*"

But when Jesus spoke on the mountain, thousands flocked to hear his words. And Jesus took the law from Moses' tablets of stone, and wrote it on people's hearts.

"*You have heard that it was said … but I say to you …*"

The people were amazed, because Jesus taught as one who had authority to show the way, not as one simply quoting others.

"*A new commandment I give to you.*"

Was this the new Moses that God had promised? The new law-giver who comes not to destroy but to fulfil?

"*If you believed Moses, you would believe me, for he wrote about me.*"

The one who brings God to the people and the people back to God? Could this be him?

Talking and Listening

Blessed are you, Lord our God,
   king of the universe,
for you spoke in former times
   though Moses and the prophets,
and in these latter days
   you have spoken through your son.

Blessed be your name for ever.

Amen.

37 Wednesday of Holy Week

The Big Story

… and Jesus said, "I am the Way", and he gave bread to the hungry, water to the thirsty and rest to the weary; and Jesus said, "I am the Light", and he brought sight to the blind, freedom to the prisoner and life to the dead; and Jesus said, "I am the Shepherd", and he welcomed the unwelcome, loved the unlovable and forgave the guilty …

Which of Jesus' sayings means the most to you?

Looking Closer

Micah 5:2-4 (NIV)

But you, Bethlehem Ephrathah,
    though you are small among the clans of Judah,
out of you will come for me
    one who will be ruler over Israel,
whose origins are from of old,
    from ancient times.

Therefore Israel will be abandoned
    until the time when she who is in labour bears a son,
and the rest of his brothers return to join the Israelites.

He will stand and shepherd his flock
    in the strength of the Lord,
    in the majesty of the name of the Lord his God.
And they will live securely, for then his greatness
    will reach to the ends of the earth.

Isaiah 61:1-3 (NCV)

The Lord God has put his Spirit in me,
    because the Lord has appointed me
    to tell the good news to the poor.
    He has sent me to comfort those whose hearts are broken,
to tell the captives they are free,
    and to tell the prisoners they are released.

He has sent me to announce the time
when the Lord will show his kindness
    and the time when our God will punish evil people.
He has sent me to comfort all those who are sad
and to help the sorrowing people of Jerusalem.
I will give them a crown to replace their ashes,
    and the oil of gladness to replace their sorrow,
    and clothes of praise to replace their spirit of sadness.
Then they will be called Trees of Goodness,
    trees planted by the Lord to show his greatness.

Engaging

Words are like suitcases. There's a lot of stuff inside.

Sometimes, of course, cat just means four-legged thing that wants to be on the other side of the door. But other times words have associations and echoes, reverberations of past uses and layers of meaning beneath a plain exterior.

Words have memories. Words bring their friends along to the party. Words have power.

John records seven times when Jesus said 'I am' with more depth than the words usually have. This is not, "Are you going to watch the football?" "I am." The Greek is emphatic, like the Hebrew name spoken to Moses. "I Am The One!"

I am the Bread of Life, the Light of the World, the Door, the Good Shepherd, the Resurrection and the Life, the Way and the Truth and the Life, the Vine. I am. Ego eimi. Ἐγώ εἰμι. אֶהְיֶה

Those who heard him knew what he was saying. When he stated, "Before Abraham was, I am", the crowds tried to stone him. When the soldiers asked for Jesus in the Garden of Gethsemane and he replied, "Ἐγώ εἰμι", everyone drew back and fell to the ground.

Words have power.

Talking and Listening

Mighty Father, Great I Am,
　the Way, the Truth the Life,

May I live my life in your light,
　May I follow your way,
　　May I know the truth,
　　　And may the truth set me free.

Amen.

38 Maundy Thursday

The Big Story

… and Jesus entered Jerusalem as the king of glory proclaiming, "The greatest one is the servant of all"; and he washed the feet of his friends, and broke bread with them saying, "This is the new covenant"; and brought into being the substance of former shadows …

What do you think Jesus meant by 'new covenant'?

🔍 Looking Closer

Psalm 24:7-10 (NRSV)

Lift up your heads, O gates!
   and be lifted up, O ancient doors!
   that the King of glory may come in.
Who is the King of glory?
   The Lord, strong and mighty,
   the Lord, mighty in battle.
Lift up your heads, O gates!
   and be lifted up, O ancient doors!
   that the King of glory may come in.
Who is this King of glory?
   The Lord of hosts,
   he is the King of glory.   *Selah*

Isaiah 55:1-9

Listen! Whoever is thirsty, come to the water!
   Whoever has no money can come, buy, and eat!
Come, buy wine and milk. You don't have to pay; it's free!
Why do you spend money on what cannot nourish you
   and your wages on what does not satisfy you?
Listen carefully to me:
   Eat what is good, and enjoy the best foods.
Open your ears, and come to me!
Listen so that you may live!

I will make an everlasting promise to you—
   the blessings I promised to David.
I made him a witness to people,
   a leader and a commander for people.
You will summon a nation that you don't know,
   and a nation that doesn't know you will run to you
     because of the Lord your God,
     because of the Holy One of Israel.
      He has honoured you.

Seek the Lord while he may be found.
Call on him while he is near.

Let wicked people abandon their ways.
Let evil people abandon their thoughts.
Let them return to the Lord,
    and he will show compassion to them.
Let them return to our God,
    because he will freely forgive them.

"My thoughts are not your thoughts,
    and my ways are not your ways", declares the Lord.
"Just as the heavens are higher than the earth,
    so my ways are higher than your ways,
        and my thoughts are higher than your thoughts."

Engaging

We now reach the final week of Jesus' earthly life, and it all starts snowballing.

I wonder how many of the adoring crowds on Palm Sunday remembered the scriptures that told of a king coming on a donkey.

I wonder how many had sung Psalm 24 the day before at the temple and recognised the king of glory.

I wonder if the disciples, as their master become their servant, understood what he had been saying for the past three years.

Talking and Listening

King of Glory,

You humbled yourself and became a servant
    to give your life as a ransom for many.
Therefore, God exalted you
    and gave you the name that is above every name.

Blessed by your name for ever.

Amen.

39 Good Friday

The Big Story

... but Passover came, and the priest became sacrifice to give life to the dead, the master became slave to redeem those in chains, and the perfect Lamb of God gave himself for the wrong of all people; and Jesus spoke forgiveness and welcomed the wanderer home; and darkness covered the land.

They thought this was the end of the story.
But it was not.

What echoes of this have we heard before?

🔍 Looking Closer

Revelation 5:6-10 (NCV)

Then I saw a Lamb standing in the centre of the throne and in the middle of the four living creatures and the elders. The Lamb looked as if he had been killed. He had seven horns and seven eyes, which are the seven spirits of God that were sent into all the world.

The Lamb came and took the scroll from the right hand of the One sitting on the throne. When he took the scroll, the four living creatures and the twenty-four elders bowed down before the Lamb. Each one of them had a harp and golden bowls full of incense, which are the prayers of God's holy people. And they all sang a new song to the Lamb:

"You are worthy to take the scroll
    and to open its seals,
because you were killed,
    and with the blood of your death
you bought people for God
    from every tribe, language, people, and nation.
You made them to be a kingdom of priests for our God,
    and they will rule on the earth."

1 Peter 2:22-25 (NIV)

"He committed no sin,
    and no deceit was found in his mouth."

When they hurled their insults at him, he did not retaliate; when he suffered, he made no threats. Instead, he entrusted himself to him who judges justly.

"He himself bore our sins" in his body on the cross, so that we might die to sins and live for righteousness; "by his wounds you have been healed."

For "you were like sheep going astray", but now you have returned to the Shepherd and Overseer of your souls.

Engaging

For thousands of years God had shown his people that sin blocked them out from his presence. God's holiness and humanity's sinfulness could not occupy the same place, and so a large curtain in the temple separated God's space from the space of the people.

Only the high priest could pass through, and only once a year, on the Day of Atonement. He entered into God's presence to offer a sacrifice for his own sin and the sin of the people. The life of an animal for the life of the people.

But on Good Friday, Jesus, our great high priest, offered his own life as a sacrifice, and by dying gave life to those dead in their sin.

The master of all humbled himself to take on the role of a slave, and with his blood bought back those in chains.

The spotless lamb of God provided himself as a scapegoat, and took away our sin to redeem all the children of Abraham.

Talking and Listening

Lamb of God,
   you take away the sin of the world.
    Have mercy on us.

Lamb of God,
   you take away the sin of the world.
    have mercy on us.

Lamb of God,
   you take away the sin of the world.
    Grant us peace

Amen.

40 Holy Saturday

The Big Story

And they carried his body to a garden and laid him in a tomb; and there was silence; and in the time between times the world waited, hardly daring even to breathe; and the Ancient of Days gathered the clouds of heaven ...

What do you think the disciples did as they waited on the sabbath?

Q Looking Closer

Colossians 1:15-17 (GW)

He is the image of the invisible God,
   the firstborn of all creation.
He created all things in heaven and on earth,
   visible and invisible.
      Whether they are kings or lords,
         rulers or powers—
            everything has been created
            through him and for him.
He existed before everything
   and holds everything together.

Daniel 7:13-14 (WEB)

I saw in the night visions, and behold, there came with the clouds of the sky one like a son of man, and he came even to the ancient of days, and they brought him near before him. Dominion was given him, and glory, and a kingdom, that all the peoples, nations, and languages should serve him. His dominion is an everlasting dominion, which will not pass away, and his kingdom one that which will not be destroyed.

Engaging

The story of God's people is a story of gardens.

It started with perfect beauty and delight, where God walked with his people in the garden, and it was good.

But in a garden Jesus was betrayed by one who was supposed to be his friend.

And in a garden his body was laid to rest.

> In this time between times, the eternal and the temporal wove a new fabric from the grave clothes, fresh clothing for New Adam and New Eve.
>
> With the eyes of eternity, God could see to the restoration of all things, when God would walk once again with his people in a garden, and the leaves of the trees would be for healing.

But with eyes fixed in time, the disciples could see only the tomb in the garden, and it was not good.

But in a garden, early in the morning …

Talking and Listening

Lord Jesus,

We find ourselves waiting,
  waiting in this time between times.

Waiting for your resurrection,
  waiting for your coming again.

Waiting for perfection, waiting for salvation,
  waiting for the restoration of all things.

In this time between times,
  we wait.

Amen.

Easter Sunday

The Big Story

... but death could not hold the Lord of Life, and in the darkness of the first day of the week, Jesus burst out and made light and life, and hope and home; and Eden is restored, Jerusalem rebuilt, and the gates of heaven opened; for the old chapter is ended

and the new chapter is begun ...

What do you think the next chapter might be?

🔍 Looking Closer

Revelation 21:1-4, 6 (NIV)

Then I saw 'a new heaven and a new earth', for the first heaven and the first earth had passed away, and there was no longer any sea. I saw the Holy City, the new Jerusalem, coming down out of heaven from God, prepared as a bride beautifully dressed for her husband. And I heard a loud voice from the throne saying, "Look! God's dwelling place is now among the people, and he will dwell with them. They will be his people, and God himself will be with them and be their God. 'He will wipe every tear from their eyes. There will be no more death' or mourning or crying or pain, for the old order of things has passed away."

He said to me: "It is done. I am the Alpha and the Omega, the Beginning and the End. To the thirsty I will give water without cost from the spring of the water of life."

Numbers 6:24-26 (NCV)

May the Lord bless you and keep you.
May the Lord show you his kindness
    and have mercy on you.
May the Lord watch over you
    and give you peace.

🧠 Engaging

It is done. It is finished.

The words of Jesus on the cross were not an admission of defeat, but a declaration of victory. The battle is over. The war is won. No more death or mourning or crying or pain, for the old order of things has passed away.

Looking around, we still see the old order. The world we live in has plenty of mourning and crying and pain, but we know that this is not how it ends. It's like we're still on the battlefield and the enemy has not got the message that the war is over.

But Jesus has conquered all. Life has risen, light has dawned, and death is vanquished for ever.

It's Sorted. It's Done.
    Accomplished. Fixed.
        Completed. Over.
            Dealt With. Crossed Off.
                Settled. Paid in Full.
                Tetelestai!
                    Τετελεσται!
                        It is Finished!

 ## Talking and Listening

Loving Father,
    Mighty Saviour,
        Guiding Spirit,

Blessing, honour, glory and power
    be yours from time to eternity.

Amen.

The Stuff at the Back

List of Readings

Genesis
1:1-5
1:20-21, 24-25
1:26-28, 31
2:8-9, 15-17
3:6-13, 22-24
15:1-6
18:1-5, 9-10a,
   16-19
22:1-13
32: 24-30
41:15-16, 25, 39-
   40
50:19-20, 24-26

Exodus
1:8-14
2:1-3, 5-7, 10
3:1-6, 9-10,13-14
6:1-7
10:3, 21-23, 27-
   28
12:21-28
12:23, 29-31
14:5-7, 10-12
16:2-4

Numbers
6:24-26

Deuteronomy
5:6-8, 11-12, 16-
   21
12:29-31
30:11-14, 19

Joshua
24:14-17

Judges
2:7, 10-11, 16-19

Ruth
1:1, 3-5, 15-16

1 Samuel
3:1, 3-10
16:1, 6-12

2 Samuel
12:1-9, 13a

1 Kings
11:1-6, 11-13
18:21, 25-27, 29-
   30, 33-38
19:4-6, 9, 11-12

2 Kings
17:12-15, 22-23

2 Chronicles
36:15-20
36:20-23

Ezra
4:1-5a

Psalms
19:1-6
22:1-2, 11-14

23
24:7-10
46:1-2, 10
51
62:5-7
91:1-6
102:1-2, 18-20
137:1-4
145:8-10, 15-16

Proverbs
3:5-12

Isaiah
9:6-7
40:1-5
43:1b-7
53:3-9
55:1-9
61:1-3

Jeremiah
31:31-34

Ezekiel
34:11-12, 14-15,
   23-24

Daniel
3:16-20, 24-25
7:13-14

Joel
2:25-29

Micah
5:2-4

Zechariah
9:9-10,19

Malachi
4:1-2a, 5

Matthew
5:1-10, 17
6:6-13, 19-21,
  24
8:5-11
10:29-31
11:2-6, 28-30
16:13-16

Mark
10:17-27
12:28-31
15:33-39

Luke
10:30-37

John
1:1-5
1:29
6:5-11, 32-35
8:31-36
14:27

Acts
7:17-19, 21-24,
  26-29
26:13-18

Romans
3:21-26
4:1-8
8:31-39
9:6-8

Galatians
4:4-5

Philippians
2:5-11

Colossians
1:15-17

Hebrews
1:1-3
11:8-12

1 Peter
2:22-25

1 John
1:8-10

Revelation
1:8, 12-18
5:6-10
21:1-4, 6

About the Author

Hi! I'm Fay.

In no particular order I am a mum, mathemagician, tea bibber, author, blogger, knitter, theology researcher, children's worker and mad scientist.

I write The Reflectionary, a weekly blog of varied lectionary-based resources for churches, youth groups, children's work and schools' ministry. Popular items are the crafts, all-age worship materials, printables and drama scripts.

Everything is free, so pop along and help yourself at www.reflectionary.org, You can sign up there to have the posts sent straight to your inbox. No spam ever, I promise!

I'm also a graduate theology student at Wesley House, Cambridge, currently researching in children's spirituality. You can find links to my published academic works at www.fayrowland.co.uk.

When not writing or studying, I teach maths for a living, and spend most of the rest of the time being creative. I worship at a large Anglican church in the English midlands, where I'm part of the teams for all-age worship and Messy Church.

I live with my children and my dragon in an untidy house full of noise and glue sticks and mess which I blame on the kids, but really, it's me.

Other Titles

A Bucketful of Ideas for Church Drama

(The Green One)

"Funny, punny, expository and engaging."

"Parables as Jesus would have told them – witty, punchy and thought-provoking."

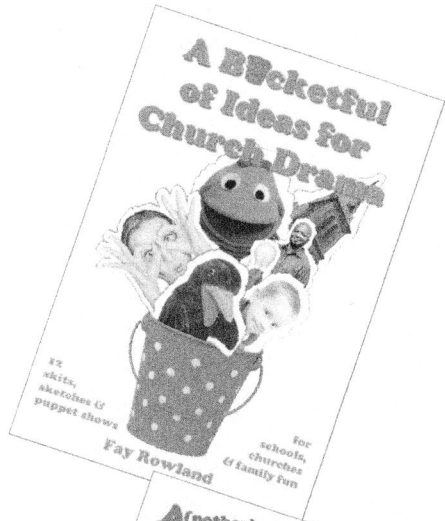

A(nother) Bucketful of Ideas for Church Drama

(The Blue One)

Including CRISP-tingle, a pop-up nativity, Abraham and his sat-nav, Jonah-Man, the pants prophet, The Stinky Son and lots more.

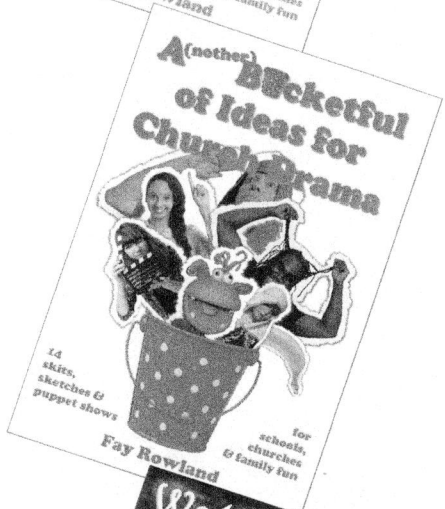

Walking to Bethlehem – An Advent Journey

25 imaginative devotions for adults and children, with reflective colouring and craft ideas.

#3 in Amazon's Advent devotions!

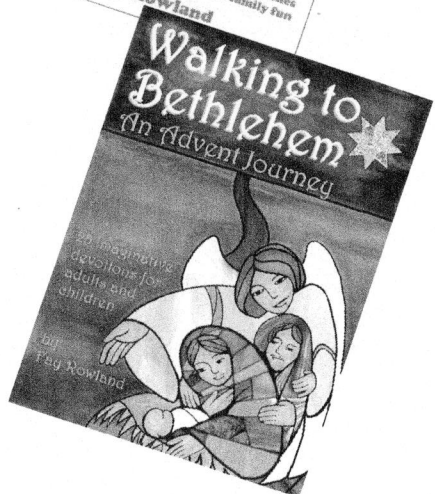

Credits

Day 1: Photo by Josh Sorenson from Pexels
Day 2: Photo from Pixabay
Day 3: The Weight of Glory (HarperOne, 2001), pp. 45-46
Day 6: *The Hospitality of Abraham* by Andrei Rublev
Day 16: Photo Marsh Williams, Pexels
Day 21: Photo by Arun Kumar from Pixabay
Day 30: Matt Redman © 2002, Thankyou Music
Day 40: Photo by Martin Marren from Pexels
Easter Sunday: Photo by Jcomp from Freepik
All other images source unknown or public domain.

Bible Credits

Bible quotations are from:

Easy-to-Read Version (ERV): Copyright © 2006 by Bible League international. Used by Permission.

God's Word Translation® (GW): Copyright © 1995 God's Word to the Nations. Used by permission of God's Word Mission Society.

The Message (MSG): Copyright © 1993, 2002, 2018 by Eugene H. Peterson. Used by permission of NavPress. All rights reserved. Represented by Tyndale House Publishers, Inc.

New Century Version® (NCV): Copyright © 2005 by Thomas Nelson. Used by permission. All rights reserved.

New International Version® (NIV): Copyright © 1973, 1978, 1984, 2011 by Biblica, Inc.® Used by permission. All rights reserved worldwide.

New Revised Standard Version Bible (NRSV): copyright © 1989 the Division of Christian Education of the National Council of the Churches of Christ in the United States of America. Used by permission. All rights reserved.

World English Bible (WEB): Public domain.

UK spellings used throughout.

Printed in Great Britain
by Amazon